Small Business Marketing

An Insider's
Collection of Secrets

ഇഇ

Michael Delaware

Published by

'If, And or But' Publishing Company
P.O. Box 2559
Battle Creek, Michigan 49016 USA

www.ifandorbutpublishing.com

ISBN-13:978-0615918570 (If, And or But Publishing)
ISBN-10:0615918573

This book contains clipart illustrations which were acquired by means of royalty free usage rights in 2013 and are copyright to: *GraphicsFactory.com* on pages: 1,5,11,15,21,27,53,109,139,163,175,185,197,205,209 & 213. All other photos and illustrations are the copyright of *if, and or But Publishing.*

While attempts have been made to verify all information provided in this publication; neither the author nor the publisher assumes any responsibility for errors, omissions, or contrary interpretations of the subject matter herein. The views expressed are those of the author alone, and should not be taken as expert instruction or commands.

To Bill & Karen Simpson

Table of Contents

ಐಲ

Introduction...1

Small Business Marketing on a Small Budget............5
Keeping Good Marketing Records...................... 11
Branding Your Business...................................15
Finding Your Customer Base............................21
The Power of Groups.....................................27
The Power of the Written Word........................53
The Power of the Internet...............................109
The Power of Reaching Out.............................137
The Power of Broadcasting..............................161
Visibility = Viability......................................173
Identity Capturing..183
Finding Places Where the Competition is *Not*.........195
Tying All the Marketing Together.......................203
A Simple 10 Step Marketing Plan to Get Started......207

Summary...211
Reference Section..213
About the Author..217

Introduction

Small business owners are commonly faced with the challenge of having to market ones company with a limited budget. Economic challenges can be tough, bleeding a company with high prices on supplies, fuel, taxation and even natural disasters.

Competition is fierce, loud and the ongoing battle for the consumer attention is unforgiving. How does one compete among the noise of so many other products and services being sold in today's marketplace? What is the best approach? The consumer or *'prospective customer'* is inundated with messages from all sorts of companies to the point where they tune out most conventional forms of advertising. How does one plan out a marketing campaign, adapt and survive under those conditions?

This book is about addressing those exact issues and concerns. It was written to empower the small business marketer with tools to go beyond the traditional ideas of just placing advertisements into the marketplace and then sitting back and hoping for the best. It is designed to help you re-think and change your mind about what works in traditional marketing approaches, as well as what works in emerging new marketing tools available.

2 ~ Small Business Marketing

To be clear, this is a book about learning to be that precise sharp shooter who delivers that specific marketing bullet right at the target prospect and then firing off those dollars with confidence followed by success. It is about conservation of resources and narrowing down the application of those resources to what is *workable* and *effective*, and learning to eliminate *what is not.*

This subject of small business marketing will be attacked from multiple viewpoints, and approaches. When this book refers to a small business throughout these pages, it assumes a business as small as one or two people all the way up to even medium size businesses of 50 or 100 people.

All such businesses face similar challenges, and all can face a bitter demise if their marketing strategies fail to achieve results. Some will have more resources than others; however, this book takes the approach of *economy* first on all forms of marketing suggested, so the methods presented here will apply to all budgets regardless of company size.

Some traditional forms of advertising will be discussed, focusing on the remaining ones that are still successful, as well as new and emerging ones too. The strategies presented here are to help the small business marketer develop a sense of a comprehensive, yet multi-faceted marketing approach that stretches the marketing dollar and strives for maximum return of those invested dollars.

The investment of *time* is also contemplated as the small business marketer's primary resource at their disposal. What can the small business marketing team do themselves to save cost, and still be effective? What are some easy and simple ways that one can begin to market and bring in new business, without a lot of upfront money?

More importantly, how does one develop an overall marketing *campaign* that reaches customers at many different levels and still stays within a limited budget? How does one begin with limited resources and then expand to having more resources for a marketing campaign, and not lose sight of what got them there?

This book takes on a challenging topic and attempts to make it easy to understand the basics of achieving results without having to spend or waste a fortune on experimentation in discovering what works. You as a reader will gain an advantage over the competition by learning from the experiences of other small business marketers who have faced the same challenges you face. This information is compiled here.

The topics that will be covered are not only maximizing resources, but also achieving viability, capturing identities, becoming visible where your competitors are not, branding, finding your precise customer base and ultimately tying all of your marketing together.

It will discuss the power of groups, print media, the internet, social media and broadcast media. This book will demonstrate new ideas to consider in reaching out within your community offering ways to achieve immediate success even if you have limited resources.

So prepare to step out of the expensive standards embedded in the conventional methods of the past, and embrace the unconventional survival secrets of a fellow small business marketing insider who has been there. Avail yourself of this collection of insider secrets compiled over four decades.

I am wishing you all the best in creating a successful, prosperous and rewarding marketing campaign

4 ~ Small Business Marketing

Small Business Marketing on a Small Budget

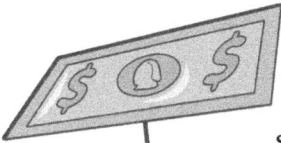

Small business owners are no strangers to economic hardships. Each and every one knows that around every corner there are surprises. These 'surprises' can range from industry changes, to personnel problems, to delayed or lost income from capricious customers. The list goes on and on.

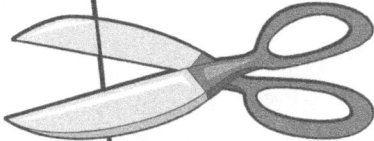

Nor is the small business owner a stranger to the concept of having to manage a business on a budget. The tax man, government regulations and the ups and downs of the economy can take a toll on the expenses of a company's pool of resources. By the same token, a small business owner knows that there are many other businesses competing for that almighty consumer dollar. There is no shortage of competition in the marketplace, and if one is not persistent, ones business will go under. That is the painful truth of small business: One must persist and survive *or die.*

Thus it is essential to be able to market and promote a business, but at the same time economic challenges can make one conservative when it comes to taking that big leap and spending money on the latest advertising campaign that presents itself. The margin for error is unforgiving. Spending money on a non-workable marketing campaign can do more damage than good. Making the wrong move can create a financial hardship rather than create good results. What is worse is that once one has failed at one marketing campaign and tried another and another to the same result, it is easy to become galvanized and resist any new information presented on the subject.

So marketing dollars spent must, must, must always result in new business. There can be very few exceptions. One can have a good company image, but if the consumers are not patronizing your business then that image can all be for nothing. So as a small business marketer, one must always be looking for that point where marketing and publicity turns the corner and becomes new or return business income.

So how does one go about conducting a marketing campaign on a small business budget? The answer is that one needs to be able to develop the skill to select tools to use in a campaign that returns far more than one invests. 'Experts' who sell advertising quite often tell business people that they should expect 1.4X to 2X the return for their one dollar invested. Some will tell you it takes a long time, and a long term commitment before you see results. The only truth in these two ideas it that they are trying to sell you advertising services over a period of time before you come the awareness of the fact that it does not work. Most of the time when some expert is telling you it takes a long time to see results; it is because the only ones who see results from that form of advertising are the larger businesses with seemingly unlimited funds to pump into it.

A small business marketer can ill afford to try to pretend to promote their company as if they had an unlimited or large budget like a mega corporation. It may sound ridiculous to think that someone would try, but you will be surprised to learn that quite often that business that closed and only lasted a year in your neighborhood was trying to do just that.

To be a small business marketer, one has to constantly adopt frame of mind that whatever marketing one does should cost as little as possible, but with maximum results. For many, this may seem like an unrealistic or impossible task, but in fact if you have run a small business it has to become a reality. Opening and operating a small business always costs far more than one originally expected when starting out. Keeping a business going takes a keenly honed survival instinct that unfortunately many do not acquire and fold prematurely.

So what kind of results should a small business owner expect? More importantly, what should a small business marketer demand as a result? Here is a basic rule to follow: If whatever you are trying as an aspect of your marketing campaign does not bring in *more dollars* than you invested (including *your time and energy*) then it should be abandoned in favor or something else that does. It does not matter how pretty the advertising gimmick is, or how much you like it, if it is not pulling in customers who buy your product you should drop it like a hot potato and find something that does compel customers to come in and buy. Time frames can vary. One should test something no longer than a maximum of three months and measure the results. If there are no results, modify it or toss it and move on.

To assume a very demanding frame of mind, one should strive for requiring marketing to pull in 5X to 10X what one invested in it in return income. That is the real ideal scene. It may seem sky high in terms of expectations, but why not? Why should you as a marketing director not be demanding? You are in charge of your companies marketing dollars, and if you do not invest those dollars wisely you will be without a company and a job soon enough. So do not be afraid to place that bar really high, and insist on performance from every corner of your marketing campaign. As a marketing director you have your hands on the vital bloodline of the company, so be insistent at all times that it works.

So the measure of success of any marketing campaign is: Does it connect with real customers who in turn buy your product? Can you measure the results in terms of sales and income, and not some popularity survey? Does it generate positive return by or before three months?

If a marketing campaign does not connect with the consumer, it is a waste. In fact one needs to go beyond the idea that one advertises and gets in a person who saw the advertisement. This is okay, but it is too small a scale. One needs to think like a three ring circus at times and try to get the marketing to simply 'Wow!' the public who sees it so that they share it with others you would not have ordinarily reached. Additionally, new marketing mediums, especially if they cost money to implement, should bring results in a timely manner or they should be abandoned swiftly.

An integral part of the success of a small business marketing campaign is trying to find the 'Wow!' factor in all that you do.   It is also examining closely what works, and keeping what does, and tossing out what does not. This book is about sharing ideas and strategies that can help you achieve the 'Wow' factor on a low budget and at the same time adhere to the tools that are working. Just like a three ring circus, one clown dancing does not 'Wow' the crowd. So one needs to include the *elephant*, the *daring trapeze,* the *balancing act* and *the lion tamer* and have them all going on at the same time seven days a week to start approaching the audience 'Wow' factor. One does not just run a single advertisement and wait. One runs the advertisement, hosts an event, sends direct mail, makes calls, hands out flyers in the community, calls a press conference, etc. One thinks like a circus, and is always looking to have as many 'acts' in motion at one time.

When I ran a small business in the Atlanta metro area I tried to emulate this concept as a marketer. I was not looking for the one week or one day promotion. I was looking for the month long, and quarter long promotion with daily and weekly 'Wow' explosions to capture the consumer's attention. I incorporated many of the techniques presented in this book, and as a result I frequently had other struggling business owners coming to me saying '*I see your business in the news all the time... How do you do it? You are everywhere!*'

This book is about finally sharing that knowledge. Whereas they were spending 3X the budget I was and getting no results, I was spending a pittance and getting the 'Wow' factor all the time and my store was always busy. One does not need an unlimited budget to get the 'Wow!' factor effect. One just needs to think like a resourceful small business marketer and maximize results from the budget you do have. Most of the marketing strategies you will find here cost very little to implement and some are cost-free entirely. They all *do* require some time commitment, but you will find it is well worth it in the long run.

The best frame of mind to develop when one sees a form of marketing one wants to include in their own campaign is: '*That is interesting, how can I do that myself for my own company at low cost or free?*' Once you really have that frame of mind, you will have traveled far along the path of comprising the proper framework for a small business marketing campaign. A good comparison is this: say you wanted to buy some fireworks. You had a budget of $20. You go to the fireworks store and see one large firecracker for $20 that creates a huge report, and another shelf that has a brick of fire crackers which has 300 smaller firecrackers with small reports for the same money? Which is going to draw more attention? One might think the one time larger explosion would, but in fact it is the series of 300 separate smaller pops being generated in a row over and over again that will draw people's attention.

Running a small business marketing campaign is very much like that. It is stretching one's budget and creating the continual small explosions capturing the consumer's attention over and over, much like a child tugs on his mothers skirt in the grocery store over and over. It is the 'hey, over here!' cry over and over again that draws the attention, not just one boom of explosion like a Super Bowl commercial.

Think about it for a moment. Can you remember any particular television commercial from the last Super Bowl as you read this? If you do, do you remember the commercial or the product? Did you go buy the product as a result? Super Bowl commercials are an example of spending money on a 'boom' and letting the echo wear off in the customers mind with no effect.

However it is the beating of the drum over and over again of the small consistent advertising campaign that begins to sink into the customers mind, and return results. This is the territory of the small business marketer. Multiple facets promoting the same message over and over again wherever the customer turns. This book is about helping you achieve that effect with your small business marketing campaign.

Keeping Good Marketing Records

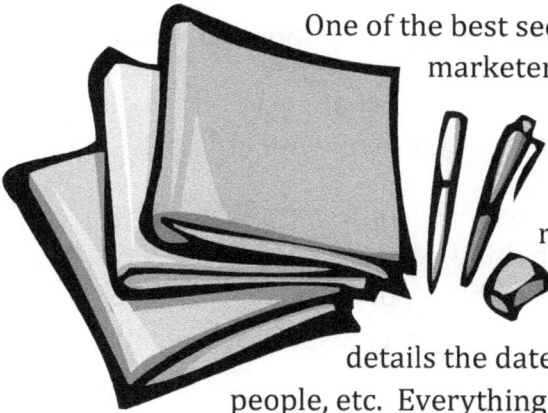

One of the best secrets any small business marketer should know is the magic of keeping good marketing records. This is essentially keeping a running record of all the moves your company makes in marketing. It details the dates, times, designs, layout, people, etc. Everything and everyone in a campaign and what was done and when.

Log Books

This information can be kept in a number of ways. One way is to keep a log book of what happened. Important things to note in a log book are:

- When an advertisement, promotion or other event was held or launched.

- How long such an advertisement was run or the promotion or event was held.

- Any special conditions about the time frame this was held. I.e. was it raining, snowing, during a big vacation week in the summer, etc?

- What was the promotion or advertisement?

- Who was working the incoming phone lines during the time it was run.

- What were the sales statistics before, during and after this advertisement or promotion was run?

- What was the outcome to note down about the results?

- Any other important information unique to that event or campaign that you might want to remember later.

Log books serve as a form of memory for the small business marketer. It is particularly helpful when one wants to repeat a successful seasonal sales event from a prior year. One simply looks up the logged information and repeats it.

Photographic Records

If you are running a business that has retail showroom or office place, keeping a regular photo record can be extremely helpful in marketing plans. One simply takes a weekly or monthly photo of the displays or overall showroom and logs it.

This is simple with digital photography these days. One can set up a free **www.Evernote.com** account or some other online storage system and store photos for each month or year in a folder, and keep a running record. This information serves as an invaluable record for repeating displays that were successful during a sales campaign, helping with recall on what was on the showroom floor during that time in terms of products, etc. Photos also help cross reference written records and pick up details that can later be recovered from studying the photos.

The Running Record

In all that we will cover in this book about the various campaigns and methods to market your small business, always keep in mind that one should keep a record of what was run before. Data back-ups of website information and blogs help with this. Also keeping copies of financial receipts for advertisements paid, as well as results achieved in any written or online form. Keep also a clipping book of newspaper articles one was successful in getting run, and make sure the date and headline are saved along with the article.

These *'running records'* help one repeat successful actions of the past, and serve as an invaluable memory for the company and any future marketer who succeeds you. In this way the legacy of all that you accomplish as a small business marketer cannot be lost.

A small business marketer in the beginning may need to create new ideas from scratch, but the longer one is on the job, provided they keep a good record system, one can borrow successful ideas from the past and repeat them. In this way one also gains the ability to isolate what works in marketing and when. Sometimes a campaign could turn out to be a good one if run at a different time of year, for example. Keeping good notes of what one learned while running it can help later.

This kind of record keeping also helps with advanced planning, especially if the small business marketer knows that the successful sales item was something that needs to be ordered two months in advance in order to have it in stock in time for the sale, etc. All of these elements and more are the benefits of having a running record of one's past efforts (both success and failures) so that one can improve the campaign going forward into the future.

Branding Your Business

Having a brand can differentiate your business from your competitors and drive customer loyalty. Do not fall into the belief that branding is just for multi-national companies with huge budgets. Small and medium companies can create an effective brand by examining how the business works, what it means to its customers and acting on the results.

Brands can be defined in two ways.

1) A brand can be identification or a mark that differentiates one business from another (through a name or a logo, for example).

2) A brand can also symbolize how people think about your business. Building a brand helps customers in their decision-making, creating a perceived knowledge of what they are going to buy - before they buy it. It is in part an image that is created of your company in the customer's mind, before they buy from you.

Brands are based on confidence in a business; product or service doing exactly what the customer already believes it will do. For example, a 24-hour convenience store brand can be based on customers' confidence that it will be open, whatever the time of day or night.

The emotional response of the customer to purchasing a product or service can also influence branding. For example, a clothing retailer can create a brand based around making its customers feel good about what they wear, how they look, how good they feel about buying clothes from that shop and what it says about them to their peers. A brand builds a unique personality for a business, and therefore attracts a defined type of customer.

Most importantly, branding is based on consistently rewarding the confidence and delivering the expected emotional response. For example, a domestic window cleaning company can build its brand successfully if customers' feel the windows on their homes are always thoroughly cleaned, the owners believe that they are using the best window cleaning company and feel good about returning to their homes and seeing the sparkling clean windows. A brand can cover the business as a whole or separate products and services.

Defining Your Brand

How does one define a brand? To begin, consider the answers to the following questions concerning your company:

- *Why do people buy from your company?*

- *What is it that makes your company different and appealing?*

- *Do you sell a particular or specialized product or service?*

- *Does your company have a specific expertise?*

- *Does a specific market group prefer to work with your company?*

- *What is your company not?*

- *What does your company not want to be?*

- *What does it want to be?*

- *What does your company stand for?*

Really mull over these answers and see if you see a pattern of ideas emerging. Branding is about how your company looks to the world. How it is seen in the market, and recognized. Brands also imbue trust for the consumer, and the effort to brand is to establish that method in which to acquire that trust and associate it forever more with that brand. This is the ideal scene ultimately.

A successful company will endeavor to make sure its branding and message is consistent across all communication platforms. It seeks to cross over many demographics, and achieve relevance.

Creating Your Brand

Creating a brand involves taking a thorough look at what your business does, what your customers will expect it to do and what image one wants to create. A brand can become an image and position the company in a particular way, such as the 'hand-made clothing store with comfortable clothing' or the 'Big and Tall fashion designer'.

Once you have worked out a brand and designed the logo or

name, or both, then survey with your customers or prospective customers. See if it is the reaction you wanted. Build the message into everything your customer or potential customer sees and hears before they have any direct contact with your business. Make sure your company literature reflects your brand values. If necessary, redesign your logo and company stationery so it provides an immediate visual link to your brand values. For example, if speed is a brand value, add an indication of movement into your company's designs.

Branding can be a great way to tie all elements of a small business marketing campaign together. The connection of the logo and the products and services within this campaign can help your company be retained in the memory of your clients. Clients cognizant of your brand and image will share it with others, and in this way word of mouth can also be bolstered through branding.

Creating and running a brand is not just something that stays on the design table and it tossed about in advertising images. Once it has been created, following some simple rules should ensure its continued effectiveness.

Always think about what your business achieves for your customers and structure your business to achieve it. Be focused on your customers' needs, but never let your customers dictate to you what your brand image it. It is your brand, not your customers'. If you change your brand values just for one customer, you will damage your brand. Do everything you can to make sure that the brand message is delivered consistently.

From company letterhead to the way the phone is answered, your customers should always feel that you are providing them with exactly what your brand promises. Keep your staff involved with your brand. More than anything else, your employees will be responsible for making the brand work. Make sure that everyone believes in it and encourage and take notice of any suggestions they may make to improve the delivery of the brand message. Your staff must understand and forward the concept of the brand to create the consistency of the image it creates.

Meet and exceed what your brand promises to customers. Failing to deliver a brand promise just once will damage your brand. Delivering your brand promise - and doing it better than your customer expects - will strengthen your brand.

Branding can bring together all the important elements of a small business marketing campaign and this cohesion can result in a rocketing of sales.

Promoting Your Brand

Once you have designed and developed your brand, it is important to make sure it is promoted in all your marketing. It becomes the tie that binds all of your efforts together. Place the brand elements such as the logo on all your online presence from a website to emails. Use it everywhere, including in your advertisements.

Also, as part of your branding it might include a phrase or motto you have worked in with the campaign. Let's take one to promote a pest control company called 'Best Pest Control'. Let's assume they designed a classy logo and added the phrase '*We create bug-free living*' as part of their marketing.

This line: '*We create bug-free living*' should be included not only in all of their print media and brochures and business cards, but also online. It also should be used in reception on the hold button and even when the reception answers the phone *"Hello, This is Best Pest Control - we create bug-free living"*.

20 ~ Small Business Marketing

This is all part of branding and getting the message out there. Any commercials on radio, television or on YouTube should also include not only the logo imagery but also the message *'We create bug -free living'.*

Branding is created in the marketing department and promoted, however it also the responsibility of the entire company to back up and promote the brand in all they do. This kind of campaign builds confidence and unity in the idea of what the brand promotes. This is how one builds a company image that aligns with the brand.

Finding Your Customer Base

To be effective in a small business marketing campaign, one must recognize that one has a base of customers that are more likely to buy your product or service than others. These 'customer bases' will vary from business to business, and although many cross over to different businesses, each is different and unique to that business. Finding one's own customer base requires that one take a little time and conducts some basic surveys.

The best place to start is with customers who have already bought from your company. Assemble a list of 10 - 20 names and call them up. Tell them you are doing a follow up on how they are doing with their product or service, and ask them if you could ask them 5 short questions.

Keep the number of questions under 10 and make them short, as people are busy and will decline to accommodate you if you do not. You need whatever information you can gather initially, so keep it short and sweet.

What is important to know? From a marketing perspective what you want to know is where they frequent, where they shop, where they use your product or service, etc. All of this information will help you find out where other people, like your customer, frequent and can be found. What you are trying to accomplish with a survey is finding other people like your customer who have similar interests, so that you can target marketing efforts to where those people are rather than just spend tons of money on broad range advertisements.

Here is a suggestion of 5 things you might want to know about your customer. Here are some suggested survey questions:

1) What are your favorite restaurants in the area?

2) What is your favorite radio station to listen to?

3) What is your favorite place to shop?

4) Do you ever make purchases online, and if so, what websites are your favorites?

5) What is your favorite use for the _____product you bought from us?

What would the above survey tell you? For one, after interviewing 20-25 prior clients it might tell you what are your customers favorite place to shop and eat in the area are. This would help you select stores or restaurants approach with some sort of cooperative advertising approach.

It would also tell you what radio station your prospective clients are listening too in the area. It would tell you what websites they buy from, and this will give you a clue as to where to advertise online.

Finally it will give you information on what they like best about your product or service, and give you're their insight into its application and use. This will also give you clues to finding new customers.

For example, let's say you own a sporting goods store and you used the above survey on the last 20 canoe sales. You discover with the last question that 12 out of 20 customers are using their canoe on a particular river outside of town. This would give you a clue as to where these people spend their time. Would it not be safe to assume that if one took some time to go explore that area, one might discover places to advertise in that area and reach new clientele? Perhaps even advertising on the buses that transport people up river from the parking area might be an original idea. It also could be there is a local hang out such as a coffee shop there, or a restaurant that one could advertise at. Doing such a survey will help you get clues to information that you might not uncover otherwise.

As an ongoing process, whenever your company makes a sale one should seek to find out how the person buying found out about the company. This is valuable information.

Another way to do this is to collect email addresses from all of your clients and then email them a survey. One can use a website such as **SurveyMonkey.com** to create free surveys and ask your customers questions that you want to know. They just click on the link you send them and answer the questions. Quite often people are bored at work and will answer emails and have time to do a survey. You would be surprised at the information you will find.

Surveying your public is an awesome way to find out information about their buying habits, places they frequent, what interests they have, etc. As a rule of thumb, a good marketer is always surveying his or her target audience and always seeking to find out more information about other target audiences they might have.

There can even be a separate target audience for different products your company sells. You will only find out this information from an active survey campaign. For example, let's assume you have an auto dealership and you sell station wagons, sedans and sports cars. You might find out through survey that the buyers of sports cars are single people or more exactly men within a particular age group.

However, let's say you were trying to resolve struggling sales with your station wagons and decided to do a survey. You discovered that these were bought by families with children, which is easy to assume without a survey. However, in your survey you discover that 70% of them were dog owners! Now that is something you can capitalize on!

The next advertisement you create for your station wagon should include a dog in it! Perhaps even a funny one with a dog at the steering wheel to catch their attention, and buy some advertising space at your local veterinarian office, pet food store, etc. Do you see how the creative juices can start to flow once you have some information about your target audience?

The 'target audience' in this example on the station wagons was not just families, but dog owners! This is the market you need to reach out to with the station wagon advertising and promotion. Pepper this kind of imagery of a dog and the station wagon on your website, radio ads and any photo you market with this vehicle, include a smiling canine friend. You might even expand your survey to find out what kind of dog a majority of those people own! Place that breed in the advertisement. Or perhaps you find they are multiple dog owners, so place two dogs in the ad choosing the top two breeds surveyed.

This is how you narrow down your customer base for your business, and its individual products and services.

Another good example of a company (which we will refer to as 'ABC Clean Up') finding their target audience. *ABC Clean Up* is a business that specializes in disaster clean up in Michigan. Their specialty is in clean up of disasters like flooded basements, backed up sewer lines, mold, water damage, etc. in residential and commercial settings. For years their marketing department launched a campaign directly at homeowners and spent a lot of money and received minimal return. The company struggled long. Finally they surveyed their customers and discovered that most of their business was coming from sources who recommended the homeowners to the company.

With this new knowledge, they decided to do more surveys. Through the additional surveys they found that insurance companies, Realtors and even city emergency service employees were the people that were in contact with a person first when they had a disaster to clean up, and those were the people who referred the business to *ABC Clean Up*. That was how a majority of people were contacting them for services.

So instead of continuing to market their services to the homeowner directly, they switched their entire marketing strategy to insurance agents, insurance claims departments, and emergency service personnel in local municipalities and joined the local Board of Realtors to interact with Real Estate Professionals. Their referral business soared, and so did their business.

Taking time to survey, survey and survey again and again is an essential ingredient for the small business marketer to discover the clues to how to reach their target audience. With constant survey actions, and always finding ways to ask people you come into contact with questions about their day to day activities, life styles and preferences one can not only find a broad target audience, but also more narrow audiences for individual products and services.

The Power of Groups

"There are basically two types of people. People who accomplish things and people who claim to have accomplished things. The first group is less crowded."

- Mark Twain

Participating in groups as a small business marketer is not only essential to connect with the community around one, it is also quite fun. The basic face to face social gathering and interchange of ideas one often discovers with participating in a group makes it worth it. Joining a group within the community is a fantastic way to reach out and have a face put with your business on a personal level. People like to do business with people, and groups help to make your business a 'people business' if you engage in participation in one that will bring you business.

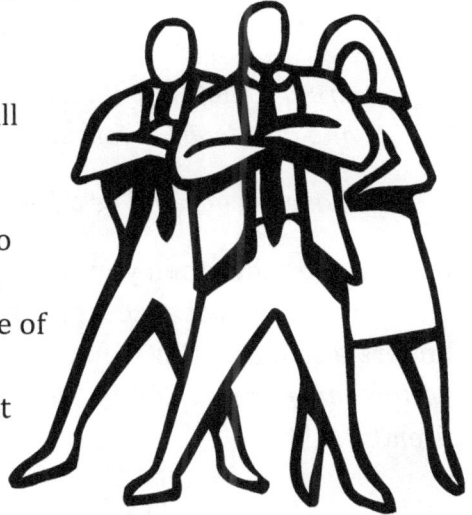

If you have ever had the experience where you tried going to a group to obtain leads or make new connections and it did not seem to work for you, then I would suggest one of two things were the case.

1) *You were in the wrong group.*

2) *You were concentrating on 'networking', 'getting future business' and 'making money' rather than making friends.*

This last part is where most people fail when they join a new group. They seek to come on strong and engage in business discussions with the other members before they have really developed a sense of familiarity or trust.

To make joining a group a success one should do the opposite of the above, and do the following:

1) *Make it your purpose to share with the group.*

2) *Bring something of value to other members. Contribute and give leads, information and time.*

3) *Make friends and be a friend to the other members.*

If you can do this, then you will have taken a big bold step into a whole new realm of success for your business and you will truly understand marketing is not 'advertising' but more so *'Raising with others personal familiarity, so business can be done among friends'.*

In the next few chapters, let's explore types of groups a small business marketer can join to expand their reach and influence, and ultimately increase income for the business.

Leads Groups

Perhaps one of the most fruitful sources of generating new customers for a business entrepreneur to explore is the participation in a Leads Group. *What is a 'Leads Group'?* A Leads Group is an organization of individual business owners and professionals who come together at regular meetings, usually over a breakfast or lunch, and share ideas and leads for each other's businesses.

The fundamental concept is that one joins the group, usually for an entry fee, and meets with other business owners or professionals. The members help each other by sharing customers. Leads Groups can become an incredible resource to obtain customers because one is not just getting a name of a customer in need of a service, one is getting *a referral* from a member of the group. A referral is so much more valuable to the business owner than just a prospect's name. A referral is essentially Joe saying '*I suggest you speak with Bill, he is who I recommend for that service or product*'.

Customers will usually not shop other professionals in your line of business once they receive a referral from someone they trust. These kinds of clients are typically the best, as the faith they have on the referrer transcends to the professional they are referring to.

What makes a Leads Groups work? Here are the key ingredients to a successful Leads Group:

- Every member brings at least one referral each time they meet for another member of the group, or provided one to another member since the last meeting.

- Members of the group socially interact and enjoy each other's company.

- In addition to sharing leads, every member has a chance to explain their business to the group at some point on the groups meeting calendar.

- Members share successes with others on past referrals

they have received. In this way all members come to see that the system is working.

- Members of the group meet frequently enough to build relationships.

What are some of the rules to structure such a group? Rules for each group can vary, but here are some of the common ones to expect:

- The group controls its membership, and only allows one category of a business to join. This means that the group will have only one chiropractor, one Realtor, one insurance salesperson, one dog groomer, etc. This way membership in the group becomes valuable, as being in the category, one receives exclusively the leads for that profession.

- The group charges fees to participate. These can be above and beyond the cost of lunch or breakfast.

- Attendance is required. One cannot remain in such a group if one skips meetings too frequently. Commonly there are rules that limit a member from skipping a certain number of meetings per month or year before they are replaced.

- One is required to bring a referral for another member of the group. Sometimes points are awarded within the membership on number of referrals given during time periods. Sometimes when a group meets every week, the requirements can be that a person must bring at least one genuine lead a month.

The groups tend to meet either weekly, every other week or on a monthly basis. Therefore participating in such a group requires a commitment.

When one begins participating in such a group, it can be easy to dismiss the value if one does not receive business immediately. Quite often membership shifts and changes in such groups with new people coming and going merely because they do not understand that the success in such participation cannot be measured on the short term.

It takes time for such participation to bring a return on investment. This is social interaction at its finest. Whenever one joins such a group, there is a slow curve of time that must pass before the results can be noticeable. Other members need time to get to know new people. Referrals come about from familiarity, trust and friendship. This takes time, and attendance at regular meetings for this to build. It does not happen overnight.

However, if one commits to joining such a group, it does require a change in ones way of thinking. Instead of thinking about one's own personal return, one must think in terms of *helping others unconditionally*. Listening throughout the week to your customers and clients for leads that might help another on your group becomes a part of life.

For example, let's assume you are a Realtor, and you hear someone at work mentioning they need a *dog groomer* for their new puppy. You should be willing and ready to take action then and refer to *the dog groomer in your group*. It may mean carrying a collection of business cards with you at the office of other members of your group, and not just waiting until the next meeting to pass along the referral. Give out the card, and then call your fellow group member and pass along the lead to them when it happens. Then when you later attend your Leads Group, you will be able to report that you referred a lead to the dog groomer that past week, and so on. If you can commit to doing this, you will be pleasantly surprised that at some point you are receiving a call or two a month from other members of your group with leads for you.

Measuring success in such a group cannot be done on the short term. It can only be measured on the long term. One must be able to give participation in such a group at least six months before one can really being to measure the results. Additionally, one cannot just measure the number of leads received, but more importantly the gross income received. After six months did you receive only one lead, but it resulted in a $40,000 sale for your business?

Let's assume participating in such a group cost you fifty dollars a month. So after six months your investment was just $300, but your return on the investment was a $40,000 sale? Imagine what it might be like after a year? What about after two years? Immediate results can sometimes happen, and you may find that in your particular industry or profession you get immediate leads. However, it is best to go into such group participation with the understanding that one cannot expect immediate return, and remain focused on the long term picture.

Some of the other benefits of participating in such a group are that you meet so many people that become lifelong friends. You can connect with the community on so many levels, and it becomes a learning experience for what is happening in the area you live and work in. It is a great way to keep your finger on the pulse of the community, and it becomes a resource of knowledge that you can share with others to your benefit.

Participating in a leads group can require a time commitment, but it can also be incredibly rewarding and develop into one of the best return on investment for your time in the long run. Quite often you will find that the customers that they refer to you, will also refer new business to you, and the chain of referrals will continue.

Service Clubs

Service clubs perhaps represent the oldest and most established organizations in Western culture. There have been many over the years that have come and gone, but there are several that remain a constant in many communities as they are connected to a national organization. Groups such as the *Rotary Club International, Kiwanis, the Optimist Club, Lions Club* and many others cross genre, gender and culture in an effort to bring professional people together to meet socially and also raise money for charity.

Here are some examples:

Rotary Club International has over 34,000 clubs worldwide. Formed over 100 years ago, Rotary has over 1.2 million members worldwide. They require a referral to join, and a commitment of attendance at regular meetings throughout the year to retain membership. They strive for high ethical business standards and practices among their members, and participation in charity efforts of the group within the community. To find out more about them visit:**www.rotary.org**

Kiwanis International was founded in 1915 in Detroit, Michigan, and became an international organization with the creation of the Kiwanis Club of Hamilton, Ontario, the following year. In the early years, members focused on business networking but in 1919, the organization changed its focus to service. In the 1960s, worldwide expansion was approved and within the decade, Kiwanis International-Europe was formed, representing Kiwanians in 11 European nations. In 1987, women officially were allowed into the membership. Today Kiwanis groups can be found in most any major city in the U.S., and throughout cities in many European countries. To find out more about them visit: **www.kiwanis.org**

Optimist International is an association of more than 2,900 Optimist Clubs around the world dedicated to "Bringing Out the Best in Kids." Adult volunteers join Optimist Clubs to conduct positive service projects in their communities aimed at providing a helping hand to youth. With their upbeat attitude, Optimist Club members help with the empowerment of young people within the community. Each Optimist Club determines the needs of the young people in its community and conducts programs to meet those needs. Every year, Optimists conduct 65,000 service projects and serve well over six million young people annually. To find out more about them visit:**www.optimist.org**

The Lions Club is another global service network with over 1.35 million members in over 205 countries worldwide. Perhaps one of the largest and oldest organizations around the globe, their focus is on community betterment projects. Each club will adopt various charity or community projects to support and raise money for throughout the year and the targets can vary regionally, however the focus remains on giving to and supporting the local community. To find out more information on the Lions Club visit: **www.lionsclubs.org**

Sertoma Inc., formerly known as Sertoma International, is an organization of service clubs founded on April 11, 1912. The name is an acronym for 'Service to Mankind'. Sertoma has clubs all over the United States and in Canada. Sertoma's primary focus is on assisting the more than 50 million people with hearing health issues and educating the public on the issues surrounding hearing health. In order to achieve these goals Sertoma has undertaken a multi-faceted approach by launching programs that address both the treatment and prevention of hearing related problems in health. For more information on them visit:**www.sertoma.org**

Junior Chamber International (JCI) is one of the biggest worldwide non-political and non-sectarian youth service organizations. It is an organization of citizens between the ages of 18 to 40 with the aim and purpose of creating positive change in the world. The organization believes that these changes must result from one taking *"collective action to improve themselves and the world around them."* Their creed does contain a religious element, however, JCI neither promotes nor engages in any religious activities. For more information about JCI visit: **www.jci.cc/.**

Soroptimist International founded in 1921 is a world-wide volunteer service organization for business and professional women who work to improve the lives of women and girls, in local communities and throughout the world. The word 'Soroptimist' was taken from the Latin words *soror* "sister" and *optimus* "best", and can be taken to mean "*best for women*". They hold the status as a non-governmental organization at the United Nations the organization claims to seek equality, peace, and international goodwill for women. The organization comprises approximately 95,000 members in more than 125 countries and territories worldwide who contribute time and financial support to community-based and international projects. Soroptimist members belong to local clubs, which determine the focus of service to their communities. To learn more about Soroptimist International visit: **www.soroptimist.org**

Apex Clubs of Australia is a network of 330 separate clubs across Australia that also focuses on community service, encouraging young people to volunteer in the community as well as develop personally. They quite often run speaking competitions and other type of events to develop life skills for young people with an emphasis on citizenship. This club was founded by former Rotary members who found some of the rules of Rotary to be too exclusionary. Up until the 1990's Apex clubs had only male memberships, but eventually changed to allow both genders in all clubs. To learn more about Apex Clubs of Australia visit: **www.apex.org.au**

As a small business owner one should seek out and join a service club knowing it is not like a leads group. However, members do share business with members and being involved with an active service club can help raise awareness for one's business in the community, and provide you with connections.

The members of the community that take an active part in a service club generally see the benefits for their companies, organization or activity in some way and therefore are willing to help others. It can also be a great marketing resource for connections into coming events in the community that can perhaps offer great opportunities for your company.

Just like with Lead Groups, referrals from one's involvement in a

Service Club can take some time and lead generation from such a group is more passive. Leads Groups tend to be more proactive with business networking, whereas Service Clubs place the purpose of the group activity before the secondary benefit of business networking. Regardless of the approach one takes, leads for business do flow on the lines of connections one can make by being involved in such a group.

It is suggested that if you have the time to be involved in both a Leads Group and a local Service Club that you enjoy, you should do so. A good strategy is to select groups that will help you connect with different members of the community that best align with your interests. This can be an important and vital strategy for a small business marketing plan to create new business and build relationships within the community. Business tends to flow smoother among familiar parties, and being an active member in a Service Club can help you make those important connections to make this happen.

Business Associations

How does being involved in a business or trade association help a business owner? Too often members of such groups neglect to attend meetings using the excuse that it is not creating new customers for them by spending time there. True, if one looks merely at getting leads from a group one is involved in as its sole value then becoming involved in a business or trade association in a profession you are a part of may not seem logical to you. Why would you want to rub elbows at weekly or monthly meetings with other Realtors or Home Builders for example, if you are a Realtor or Home Builder?

Thinking along those lines, one can slide into thinking one dimensionally and conclude that because a group does not offer leads or referrals, one should not participate. However, it may surprise you that quite the opposite is true. One can receive benefits for one's own marketing by being actively involved in a trade association or business group.

When one becomes involved actively in such a group it offers one higher professional status as perceived by members of the community. When one becomes the President, Committee Chairman or Board Member eventually in such a group, the recognition expands beyond the parameters of the just the group itself. It becomes something one can add to one's own advertising and credentials. Just this aspect alone can be an extreme benefit in giving you the professional edge over your competitors.

However, despite this kind of status benefit, this is not the main benefit of such involvement. The reason being involved in a professional business association or trade group is a vital aspect of a marketing plan is that these groups quite often become the industry reference point for the community at large.

Major changes coming in the industry from government regulations, incentives and even future community development projects generally arrive onto the communication lines of such a group before others in the industry hear about it. When one is actively involved in such a group, quite often you can be among the first to know important changes in the industry that are coming and because of this information resource one can use it to their own advantage.

Part of the success in any marketing plan is not only being able to reach new people and raise the awareness of one's own products and services. It is also staying ahead of the competition and being on the cutting edge before your competition has figured out how new developments can be an advantage.

One should look at involvement in a business or trade association as keeping one tuned into the pulse of the industry. Placing oneself into the information highway of industry changes is essential to knowing what is going on. If one waits for it to show up in the news, it is too late. Business groups and trade associations quite often knew about the forthcoming changes that are in the news today many months before other people did. If you are involved in these groups, they are quite eager to hand out responsibilities to others and share leadership over time. This can be a great way to put you and your business in a position of hearing the news first.

With having a better prediction on coming changes in the industry in which you work one can prepare and adjust your marketing strategies to align with these trends. Additionally it can help to make you a resource for information for your customers, and in so doing enable you to create a word of mouth campaign positioning your company as the resource for the answers to consumer problems in your industry.

Trade and business associations often offer referral and advertising benefits for their membership as well. Chambers of Commerce in a community if organized and run well can offer membership promotion in the community, inclusion in discounted advertising programs and also open the door to contacts within the community that would otherwise be hard to come by. The longer a business is involved and a member of such groups as the Chamber of Commerce, quite often the benefits and community name recognition stand.

There are also small business advocacy groups that can be quite helpful, such as the National Federation of Independent Businesses (NFIB or **www.NFIB.com**) who are a collective lobbying group in Washington that look out for the interests of small businesses. These organizations can also open doors to contacts that help individual businesses in their community for marketing and exposure. As a small business owner, it always advisable to be careful about introducing too much politics into the workplace, as sometimes it can work against a marketing plan. However, there are many issues that one can support openly that are beneficial to the public, and therefore can put your business in a positive light if you support it.

In short, business and trade associations can be a valuable resource for information to strengthen a small business marketing campaign. They can also serve as a means to make contacts within the community that can be advantageous to building a positive image for your company.

Volunteering Groups

Volunteering one's time within the community one works can also fit into one's marketing plan. How could volunteering accomplish this? It helps you meet people and bring awareness to your business through social means. There are many ways to volunteer in a community. The most important rule of thumb to follow is to only volunteer when you are interested in the activity and are willing to follow through.

Signing up as a volunteer and not showing up or following through can work against you in the sphere of public relations. There are many ways to volunteer within a community. It is best to first assess what your own interests are, and then try to seek out a volunteer activity that aligns with that.

Consider the following examples:

> *If you like to work with animals, how about do some volunteer work with the local animal shelter?*

If you like to work with children, how about volunteering to tutor kids after school? Or how about coaching a little league baseball team?

Every community will have different activities available, and there can be many needs that are needed. Always seek groups that will allow you to participate and then find ways to tie in your business actions to the organization you are helping.

If you decide to coach little league sports team, how about having your company name on the uniforms?

If you own a restaurant, how about have all the kids and their parents over for an 'after the game' meal?

There is nothing wrong with shameless promotion when it comes to volunteering, and people come to expect it and are most of the time happy for the contribution. Quite often so few people volunteer usually that these groups seldom turn people away. Just be sure to follow any rules they may have on the matter, and don't overdo it or it can make you appear insincere and this will work against you.

Here is a list of suggested groups one could look for in the community to get involved as a volunteer:

- Church groups

- Sports teams (baseball, football, soccer, basketball, volleyball, hockey, etc.)

- Food banks

- Homeless shelters

- Animal shelters

- Highway/Roadway Litter Clean up organizations

- Gardening groups

- A local hospice

- The local hospital

Here is a list of some National Organizations (websites included) which often have local groups within your community or in a region to help people:

Habitat for Humanity: *www.habitat.org*

Big Brothers, Big Sisters: *www.bbbs.org*

Meals on Wheels Association of America: *www.mowaa.org*

Foundation for a Drug Free World: *www.drugfreeworld.org*

International Student Exchange: *www.iseusa.com*

The American Red Cross: *www.redcross.org*

The Salvation Army: www.salvationarmy.org

Good Will Industries: *www.goodwill.org*

There are many National and International organizations that help animals. Here is a selection of some of the larger ones:

Save the Elephants: www.savetheelephants.org

Elephant Nature Foundation: www.elephantnaturefoundation.org

Black Hills Wild Horse Sanctuary: *www.wildmustangs.com*

Wild Horse Sanctuary: www.wildhorsessanctuary.org

Return to Freedom American Wild Horse Sanctuary:*www.returntofreedom.org*

Manatee Observation and Education Center: *www.manateecenter.com*

National Audubon Society: *www.audubon.org*

Bird Studies Canada: *www.bsc-eoc.org*

National Wildlife Rehabilitators Association: *www.nwrawildlife.org*

Forest Animal Rescue Wildlife Sanctuary: *www.forestanimalrescue.org*

Cat Survival Trust: www.catsurvivaltrust.org

Cheetah Conservation Fund: *www.cheetah.org*

Animal and Wildlife Area Research and Rehabilitation (AWARE): *www.awaretrust.org*

Earth Watch Institute: *www.earthwatch.org*

Cercopan Primate & Rainforest Protection: *www.cercopan.org*

Save the Chimps: www.savethechimps.org

GVI Wildlife and Terrestrial Conservation: *www.gviusa.com*

Hawai'i Wildlife Fund: *www.wildhawaiiorg.com*

The Reef Ball Foundation: *www.reefball.org*

Global Volunteer Network:
www.globalvolunteernetwork.org

Wetlands International: *www.wetlands.org*

Ocean Conservation Society: *www.oceanconservation.org*

Rico Barry's Dolphin Project: *www.dolphinproject.org*

Whale and Dolphin Conservation (WDC Society
International): *www.wdcs.org*

So as one can see, there are many, many organizations and places one can volunteer at to contact people within a community. One can achieve the fulfillment of helping worthwhile organizations, and at same time experience some positive exposure for your small business.

What if you do not have the time to volunteer? Perhaps your company should consider sponsoring one of these groups, or one of your own choosing.

One can raise money through sales in your business, and promote that a percentage of the sales goes to support your named charity organizations. One can also tie in advertising and other marketing to include a reference to the campaign your company is running to bring about good exposure.

Sponsoring a non-profit charity should be something every small business should consider. Sometimes it can make the difference between a customer spending money with your company or the competition. Whenever one makes a donation to a charity, one should take photos of a check being presented and include that news story in other marketing efforts which we will discuss more on later in this book.

So volunteering really has two separate halves.

1) *One can directly volunteer.*

2) *One can raise money through sponsorship.*

Here are some important things to consider when choosing a charity or non-profit organization to support:

If one is volunteering time, be certain it is an organization that you can follow through on your commitment with and not lose interest.

Be absolutely certain that you feel good about the organization you are supporting and do your homework.

Never support an organization that you do not feel good about, believe in or know enough to be able to talk about socially with others. It is better to choose one that you have some familiarity with rather than just a random one because it is available.

Try to select an organization that somehow ties in with the products you are selling or the services you deliver. I.e.: If you have a construction business, you might do well with Habitat for Humanity. If you have a children's clothing store, you might do well with any form of children's charity organization. If you sell furniture, you might do well with a 'protect the rainforest' organization, etc.

Volunteering and sponsoring charities and other non-profit organizations can help you receive positive exposure for your company and is easy to implement as part of one's marketing campaign. One can also receive some great personal fulfillment from helping such groups, and this too can boost your personal spirit in your business. Additionally it can open the doors to connecting with a lot of potential customers, as well as offering good positive press and exposure in local news and the internet for your company image.

Be certain to include in your marketing strategies the supporting of a local charity or volunteer organization either through first hand involvement or sponsorship, and you will see the positive benefits in the long term.

Online Social Groups

How can utilizing online social groups fit into one's marketing plan? Is it possible to really turn people into customers who you only meet through the internet? Yes, it really is possible. Businesses are doing it every day.

Consider the last time you made a purchase online. Somehow you became comfortable enough to make that purchase without going into a store, correct? People interact and learn about products and services online in the same way they do in person face to face. In fact, they do it 24 hours a day online. If you can provide the information they need, your answers will reach them whenever they log in.

Many approaches in online marketing will be discussed throughout this book. There are several ways to do to meet people online. Let's look at some of the proven ways in this chapter.

Interact and Answer Questions

If one has such a limitation on time that attending a live meeting of a group is challenging to maintain, there is always online social groups that one can participate in.

These types of groups, depending on the platform of their format usually are available 24/7 and one can log in when one chooses. Quite often they are set up where you can post a comment, question or suggestion and others can post their responses later when they log in.

One can also answer other people's questions as it relates to a topic. The best way this works for small business marketing is to answer questions about a topic that your company in some way resolves for customers. One does not need to be overt about it, or get into a *selling* mode. In fact, most of these groups discourage that behavior and have rules against it. The best way is to have your name and business in the signature line of your comments, even if it means writing it in separately each time.

For example:

> Let's assume that you are in the business of providing lawn care services. Try joining a group that is for home improvement, preferably one that is consists of members in your geographic area or region. Then, look for consumer questions about lawn care or some related topic. Answer their questions without promoting yourself, just simply include your name, business name and either an email or website in the signature of your response.

Websites such as **www.trulia.com** and **www.zillow.com** encourage Real Estate agents and Real Estate related professionals to answer questions for the public online. One can answer specific questions about the community you service, and in so doing quite often pick up prospective clients. These websites do not discourage this kind of promotion, and in fact encourage this interaction.

To find forums related to the topic of your business, go to your search engine browser and type in the name of your product or service plus the word 'forum' after it and see what comes up. If none exist, try varying the wording. If after searching you do not find a forum that satisfies your interests, then you might consider starting your own.

Set Up Your Own Forum

So what is a forum? An internet forum, or message board, is an online discussion website where you and your visitors can hold conversations in the form of posted messages. These messages can then be viewed at any future time, even if you were not online when they were posted.

Forums are a great way to foster interaction, discussion, and improve customer loyalty. They also allow you to build a following and reach out to new people in your online community, which can be tied in or affiliated with the region or area where your business is located too.

If you want to reach your own customers, and connect with new ones related to your industry you might also consider starting your own forum for this. An easy website to get started with this is:**www.forums.com**. The service is free, and they offer an easy-to-use hosted forum and discussion board platform, where you can either join in with one of their existing communities or alternatively start and build your own online community with their free forum hosting package.

Another free service for creating your own online forum is:**www.websitetoolbox.com** which enables you to build your own forum and add it to your website, etc. Companies such as Greyhound, Samsung, the American Red Cross and even Cornell

University use this service to host forums for their websites.

This product can also allow you to connect the forum with social media, build SEO for the topics and organize events online for interacting with your customers.

There are several other websites that you can explore that can also help you start your own forum. Here are a few other examples:

www.ning.com - Helps you start your own forum, but they do eventually charge fees.

www.yuku.com - Helps you start your own forum, social network and social community.

www.proboards.com- Offers the service of creating your own forum and message board.

Most of these types of services offer customizable appearances for your forum, and they offer different features. It is recommended that you explore a few of their websites and contact them directly with any questions before deciding on the right one for your business.

Online social groups and forums do require that you are active with them to make them work for your marketing campaign. This means that you need to be committed to logging in regularly to answer questions, moderate and spend time online promoting the forum. Usually once a day minimum is what is needed to keep it fresh and active. Once word of mouth spreads on the forum, it can take on a life of its own if the topic is in high demand and people discover that they can go there for answers.

If you are going to include this as part of your online marketing strategies, it is recommended that you assign a person to managing it that is committed to keeping the content fresh and active and build up the memberships. Otherwise, it can become a form of anti-marketing if people find it and no one answers their questions and the forum is not moderated as promoted.

Creating a Safe Forum for Your Customers

The other thing about forums that comes into play is the dishonesty of scammers and other subversive types online that want to take advantage of others. As much as a majority of decent people want to believe that all people are honest, it is an unfortunate truth that there are some that are not. These few see no problem in ruining a good thing for everyone else.

The best way to address scammers and criminals from ruining your forum is to maintain common security protocols when online. Never click on links sent from unknown sources, and never give out financial information online. Do not allow people to post unrelated links or unrelated topics on the forum. Set the rules and follow them. Educate your forum members on the rules and encourage them to report this kind of malicious activity so you can block these people from the group.

Obviously as a business marketer you will want to promote your products and services, and you should. Place an ad on the page of your forum and make it visible. If you can set up a website to sell your product, direct them there and have them place an order online. Or if they insist on doing business outside of the website, then get their phone contact information and contact them directly and have them come into your place of business.

A common operating profile of scammers online is that they attempt to acquire your bank wire information or PayPal information for large purchases. One common clue is that they never provide a working phone number, and avoid all direct contact in person. They also quite often want to do business 'internationally' and have you send or product money overseas in all kinds of scams.

One great resource to gain an understanding about how online scammers operate it to go to **www.craigslist.org** read about the current scams discovered by craigslist. They are usually offer the most current news about these scammers and it will help you gain an understanding on how to protect your company, your customers and other forum visitors so that you can effectively keep your forum policed and block these criminals.

Don't be afraid to expose a scammer in the forum and let others know when you catch them. These criminals hate to have their games exposed. Your customers will appreciate it too. The information on scams page at craigslist also offers resources on how to file a complaint and report fraud in the U.S. and Canada. Be sure to use this when you encounter is and help others so we can all work together to clean up the internet from these predators.

Summary

Online social groups and forums can be a great way for your business to meet new prospective customers and draw them into your business. Encourage your existing customers to participate in any forum you establish, and ask them to refer their friends and family members.

Become a resource for answers related to your business, and solve people's problems and you will have another great tool in your marketing strategies. Make the forum safe for your customers and unsafe for criminals.

The Power of the Written Word

"A written word is the choicest of relics. It is something at once more intimate with us and more universal than any other work of art. It is the work of art nearest to life itself. It may be translated into every language, and not only be read but actually breathed from all human lips; -- not be represented on canvas or in marble only, but be carved out of the breath of life itself."

- Henry David Thoreau, *Walden*

There are many ways to market with the written word. One can use print or the internet. The small business marketer can ill afford to neglect some of the traditional forms of marketing, but at the same time they must also be cost conscious in doing so, as printing can be quite expensive.

The following chapters will explore ways to make print advertising work for your budget, and attempt to direct you to what tends to be more successful than others.

Display & Print Advertising

Print as a means of advertising has long been a tool used by man. It could be said to go back to Egyptian hieroglyphics or stone carvings at its origins, moving forward in time to the development of the printing press. Mankind has long used the written and printed word to promote the events of the day, and this also included using it as a vehicle for selling goods and services. Let's examine some of the effective tools still at the disposal of the small business marketer in print.

Print Newspapers

Many forms of printed newspapers are fast becoming a thing of the past. Traditional forms of advertising are giving way to the internet, where people spend so much of their time. Readership in print newspapers are declining more and more, and many are the reading fodder of the bored travelers on airplane rides and subways who lack a mobile device in many communities.

However, there still exist newspapers and other forms of printed products that offer display advertising. With this in mind, it would be helpful to at least know some basic successful actions on what types of display and print advertising still works. Some small businesses can still do very well with such a medium, so let's examine what is the most effective for the small business marketer.

Large print newspapers will be all too happy to accept money from a small business and propound that the large circulation of the newspaper will get them higher exposure to prospective clients. Wishful thinking aside, it never seems to work, although many small businesses will toss money in the direction of the large newspaper because it seems to offer the biggest bang for reaching people.

The best measure for a newspaper from the viewpoint of a marketer is not what their circulation is, but what their actual readership is. There is a very big difference between *circulation* and actual *readership*. How do you determine this? There are many ways to gauge this. Here are three key tidbits of advice to use in examining the readership of a newspaper:

- ***Does the newspaper, large or small, publish a decent sized classified ad section?*** A newspaper can boast readership through large circulation, however, if the classified ad section is tiny it is usually a good indicator that no one goes to that newspaper when they are looking to buy something. It also indicates that the newspaper cannot sell things for people through classifieds, and therefore struggles in selling this type of ad space. A large newspaper with a small classified section quite often is less read than a smaller one with a large classified section.

- ***Are people responding with letters to the editor?*** Are the letters consistent with local topics, or do they seem canned? A well read newspaper will generate responses from their readership, and this can also be a good indicator of what types of people are reading that newspaper.

- ***Are other small businesses similar in size to your own advertising in this newspaper regularly?*** This may take some time to monitor, but it is always good advice to look before you leap. Get copies of the same newspaper and look for the consistency of other advertisers over a period of at least a month. It also does not hurt to call some of these advertisers and ask them how long they have run the ad and what results they have experienced.

It is always an advisable standard practice to round up copies of every newspaper in the area and compare them to the above three pieces of advice before you spend money. One should also take careful notes of what sized ads the successful ones are running, and where they are placing them. Placement of a display ad in a newspaper has the following variables to consider:

- Size of the ad

- What page it is located on

- What section it is in (i.e. inside the front table of contents, sports, home & garden, local news, national news, etc.)

- What side of the page it is on?

- Is it on the inseam? (This usually the section where one opens the paper and sees the staples. This can be a good location as it is usually the pages that will be displayed if it is left open on a counter somewhere because it will stay open more easily.)

- The dimensions of the ad being run

- The height of the ads placement on the page

- Whether or not color is used in the ad, or if it is just black and white

- Is a graphic, drawing or photo used in the ad?

- What does the copy look like?

- How readable is the ad?

- What does it promote as a point of contact (i.e. Phone number, address, website, email, etc.)

- What are the readers prompted to do in the ad? (i.e. Visit to a location, call a phone number, visit a website, send a text, buy a product, etc.)

You will find that when you study a publication there is a lot to learn about the effectiveness of an advertisement. A small business marketer who studies existing newspapers and does research will have greater success in choosing the right newspaper to advertise in, and what to advertise.

Phone Directories

Display advertising is not just limited to the newspapers. There is also the local phone directory. Certainly large phone books in major metro areas are disappearing, and getting smaller. However, quite often in small communities or counties, the smaller phone directories are still in existence and are still used. Remember that the older generation grew up on phone books, and despite the resources of the internet, many people in that generation still prefer to use one. Their dollars spend just as well as everyone else.

Once again in considering a phone book, it is better to choose a smaller one that covers a market area where your business services. What is most important with using a small phone directory as a means of advertising is to choose the right category or categories for your business to be listed under.

The best suggestion is to do a careful study of an existing phone book, and see where you competition is placed in the directory.

Then seek out categories where they are not listed, and make note of them. Quite often when you purchase an ad from a phone directory printing company, they offer you additional listing placement categories in addition to your display advertisement.

Taking some time to do a survey on your customer base and ask them questions such as *'How would you best describe this product'* and show them photo. One can also ask them directly *'What category comes to mind when you want to search for _____ product?'* This kind of information can be invaluable and may also offer up categories that you had not considered listing your business under on the phone directory.

If you are posting a display advertisement in one section of the phone directory, make sure you also include the writing *'See our ad on page__'* in all your other listings in the book. This will help drive them to your ad and get more information.

What is important to note, however, is that if you place your display advertisement in a section alongside all of your other competitors, this can work against you. So it is better to choose an unconventional location for your display ad and direct people there where they will not be comparing your ad to other similar product or service providers.

For example: If all the plumbing companies place their display advertisements under 'Plumbing' try placing your display advertisement under 'Home Remodeling' or 'Hot tubs' etc. The rule of thumb in small business marketing is: *to try to be seen where your competition is not.*

It does not mean that you do not place a listing in the 'plumbing' section. What it means is that your display advertisement is your best presentation so place it where others are not shadowing you. Try to place it where you will be the only one seen in that category whenever possible.

Specialty Display Advertising

There are several other places a small business might consider placing a display advertisement. Local restaurants often sell advertising on placemats, for example. Elementary and high schools will often sell advertisements for various publications for school events such as theatrical presentations and sporting events. There are also companies that publish and distribute flyers door to door.

When considering the purchase of any unusual or untried advertising medium, as a small business marketer, you quite often need to be frugal with the dollars you spend. The best rule of thumb with any of these types of ads is the do the following:

- Ask for a copy of a previously published flier, booklet, placemat or whatever if it exists.

- Make calls to other advertisers on that publication and find out what results they achieved from it.

- If it is a new publication that has never been done before, verify the distribution and circulation of the item, and negotiate a lower rate for: *'helping them get the publication started'*. Do it as a one time trial if the price is right, and you feel good about the distribution, and monitor the results.

Billboard Advertising

Billboard advertising can be quite expensive and require a long term commitment. Unfortunately the results from such advertising are questionable, as one is essentially paying for an 'impression' of approximately 3 seconds for your brand or product when people drive by. This can work best with promoting a location such as a large casino, amusement park or zoo.

However with the small business marketer, there is one strict golden rule for this type of advertisement: *Unless you can purchase placement with a billboard along a highway that is in a location where you can include the words 'This Exit' in the ad, don't do it.*

In other words, unless your business is located in a place that is easily accessible from a major highway or corridor where that 3 second impression as they drive by can result in the prospective customer pulling off the exit to come find you, you are better off spending your marketing dollars elsewhere.

This may sound harsh, but it is a practical truth. Billboard advertising has limited effectiveness. Whenever one is spending marketing dollars for a business, one needs to see sales of the products or services one is selling. Billboard advertising can flank an existing marketing campaign, but should not be relied solely upon to launch one unless one can effectively use the words *'This exit'* in the display.

If one pays attention the next time you drive down a major highway, look at the billboards. What happens to you after you have seen the billboard the first time? Do you notice it the second or third time? Were you compelled at any time to take action on what you saw? In answering these questions you will likely discover the awareness that billboard advertising draws you to something when you are looking for a place to pull off the highway to eat, visit an interesting place or shop only. With all else the typical response is 'oh, that is interesting' and after that one tunes it out the next time it is seen.

Sometimes you may find you are thinking *'Oh that is interesting, I will have to remember to look up that website later when I get home...'* and then seldom ever do it.

This is because billboards are 3 second advertisements designed to prompt action. It is difficult to write something down or access the internet when one is driving. So unless you are a bored passenger, you are unlikely to telephone, access a website or even text when you are driving as it is dangerous and often illegal. However, when a billboard reads *'This exit'* all one has to do is turn on the blinker and then turn the wheel when the exit comes up.

Other variations on *'This exit'* may also work, such as *'Exit 365'*, *'In 10 miles at Exit 12'* or *'In two exits'* however, with these one is hoping that the their attention remains constant that long and they will act upon it as they get farther down the highway. It is an impulse driven response that comes from this type of advertisement, and there can be other distractions and temptations before they actually get to your designated exit if it is farther down the road.

If using this method, it is best to do two or three billboards in a row that keeps the reminder going as they get closer. This can often be a deadly effective approach if you have the budget, especially if one is marketing a restaurant or other food resource.

Summary of Display & Print Advertising

The best rule of thumb for this type of marketing is to look before you leap. Investigate what others are doing, and whenever possible contact other small businesses and even your competitors to see if you can find out any results they are having with it. Also look for other businesses of a similar size to yours that are remaining constant with a particular form of advertising.

Examine this one method further, as it most likely is working for them and you may want to mimic or repeat what they are doing. If you explore it more closely, you might find they are hoarding gold in a private gold mine of marketing exposure, and you might be able to copy their approach and adapt it to your marketing plan.

As another final note, sometimes one can share costs with another advertiser in the same ad space. This is called *cooperative advertising* and it is another way to stretch your marketing budget by sharing the expense with another company.

Classified Advertising

Classified advertising for small businesses is quite often overlooked as a form of advertising. However, if one assumes the viewpoint of a buyer for a moment, where do they most often go when they are looking to purchase some times of items? Certainly with the age of the internet, classified advertising has changed and there are a lot of opportunities online as well. Both online and in news print are still good places to reach prospective buyers.

One does have to be wise on how they go about their ad, in order to make it work. What one is trying to do with classified ads is to spark that phone call or email, and connect with the prospective customers.

Let's examine the two different approaches with classified advertising, and cover some basic secrets that can save you a lot of money with experimentation.

News Print Classified Advertising

Stay away from large newspapers. Focus on small local papers, particularly ones that carry a lot of local community news and events. You are looking for that weekly or bi-weekly newspaper which usually has been long established in the area and carries the good news that people are looking for. Quite often the smallest newspaper in town is the most well read, as opposed to the larger more established daily papers.

These small newspapers carry stories that feature people's kids, and themselves doing things in the community. They pick up the newspaper and share it with others showing them the article, and thus the newspaper receives its true 'circulation' at a whole new level.

When composing a classified advertisement, keep your message simple. Cover a description of what you are selling, be it a service or product, but do not get too wordy. Include the most important information which is a telephone number and/or email address. You can also include a website, but when it comes to news print advertising the phone number is quite often the information a prospect who is interested will most likely take action on.

Make sure your vital information in the advertisement stands out above the other print. For example, your phone number is a vital piece of information in the advertisement. Make sure it is larger in font size, and bold and readable above all else. Centering it in the column of the ad also helps to make it stand out.

Make sure you have an attention grabbing headline for the

advertisement. Have this be in bold and a larger type style above the rest of the print.

It is important to note that the headline should communicate the service or product that a person might be looking for, and this may or may not be your company name.

Study the other ads and see what similar products are being advertised and see how they are writing their ads. Quite often when you look at a newspaper week after week and see the same ads in there, it is easy to determine which ones are drawing attention. The ones that are continually there are quite often well written ads that are creating prospects for the advertiser running them.

When you place an ad, and get no response, adjust the content. Change the headline; change the wording, the placement or location in the newspaper, etc. When you place an ad and it gets a response, keep running it and don't change what is working.

Sometimes you run an ad and it works great for two to three weeks, and then runs cold and you get no calls after. What you have to realize it that you may need to run this type of ad as an alternate one.

Try pulling the ad for a month, and run another one in its place, then run this one again in 30 days. It may be that it starts giving you calls again once it has been out of the classified section for a month or so. You can also try running the ad in a different section of the newspaper to capture more attention. You may also find that the ad is a seasonal ad, and it best run during the summer and another copy works better for the autumn or winter, etc. Making regular adjustments to classified advertising helps to keep the message fresh, and capture attention. Just be careful not to carry too far from the main theme, and don't change something if it is working. Only make changes when it stops working.

Online Classified Advertising

As the internet expands, there are many places online to sell goods and services through the means of classified advertising. With each passing year, more and more people are going online to search for things that they traditionally went to the newspaper for in the past. These types of websites featuring classified ads have grown to become a popular resource for the online shopping consumer, as it is a matter of convenience.

Here are few of the popular websites they frequent:

Craigslist

The most common resource for online classified advertising is: *Craigslist.com*. Posting a specific classified advertisement about a product or service you provide within your community can be a great way to connect with new prospective clients. Craigslist started out as a small email distribution list to friends by a man named Craig Newmark in the San Francisco Bay area in 1995 featuring local events in the city.

It became a web-based service in 1996, and expanded to include classified advertising following its web-based establishment. It started expanding to other cities in 2000, and currently covers 50 countries around the world and helps people sell goods through classified ads in seven languages including English.

Craigslist has its benefits and its negative aspects too.

Craigslist benefits = your business can reach a target audience in a specialized geographic area and post it in a specific category that will be seen by buyers shopping in your area and in that category.

Craigslist negatives = Spammers and scammers frequent craigslist and will respond to your ad in an effort to obtain your financial information or connect with your PayPal account. To be alert for these criminals, you need to familiarize yourself with the section posted on craigslist entitled 'Avoid Scams & Fraud' and also the section on 'Personal safety tips' whenever doing business on Craigslist.

Whenever selling as a business on Craigslist, you need to identify your ad as a business rather than as an individual to conform to their rules. Simply choose this setting when placing your ad.

E-Bay

Ebay.com is another great means to sell specific goods and services online. They are the largest and most well established online service for selling individual items and products in a classified or display advertising format online.

E-Bay requires that you set up an account with them, and if you are going to sell as a business you will be required so set up a business account. To sell an item on E-Bay they charge an insertion fee and a final value fee calculated on the value of the sale when the item sells. The insertion fees can vary depending on account status.

With E-Bay your first 50 items you list for sale each month are free. Beyond that number you pay a fee. You also pay a fee when the item sells. The sequence for selling an item on E-Bay is to:

- *List it*

- *Sell it*

- *Ship it*

- *Get paid*

To find out how to get started, search for '*E-Bay Quick Start Guide*' on your search engine or **click here**.

Etsy

Etsy.com is more of a niche market resource for selling online items though a classified or display format much like E-Bay. Their rules are similar in terms of how they operate to E-Bay. Etsy tends to focus on the creative businesses and has a specific group of buyers.

Etsy allows the sales of handmade goods, Twenty years of older vintage goods and craft supplies only.

There is no membership fee. The charge 20 cents (.20 US) to list an item for 4 months, and they charge you a 3.5% fee when the item sells.

These costs need to be factored into your profit margin whenever you consider using this service.

Amazon

Amazon.com is another great resource to sell your products. They charge a monthly fee of $39.99 to businesses, and also a fee when the items sell. They do not require a long term commitment, and the first month is usually free with their online promotion.

However, this kind of commitment for your business might be better off being used once you know that your product is tested in the marketplace. Trying it out for free for the first month on the other hand may be a great way to see if your products have broad appeal.

This may not work for every business model starting out. For more information, visit:
www.services.amazon.com/sellingoneamazon

Shopify

Shopify.com is similar to other online classified advertising stores you can use. They allow you to sell your products and services in your own created online store much like E-Bay. Their fees for their introductory basic plan are $29 a month and they charge a 2% transaction fee on items you sell. With their basic plan you can post up to 100 items for free and use your own domain.

Summary

There are many other services for setting up your own online store in a classified ad format. Each one varies in their costs and exposure to prospective buyers. When exploring one of these services, try them out initially and see if you get any kind of sales from them. If you do, it might be worth expanding your commitment and investing more time and energy into it.

Small Newspapers

Small newspapers as I mentioned in an earlier chapter are quite often better read than larger newspapers. However, one should do their own independent research on each paper to find out which ones are particularly popular in an area, as not all small newspapers are well read.

Small newspapers also offer many advantages than larger ones do not. They quite often carry local human interest stories and happenings in the community. They are also great resources for running local articles about small businesses getting involved in the community. Quite frequently they are looking for topics to print stories about, so this can offer an opportunity for exposure if one takes the time to write the story and present it to them.

What are the advantages of getting a story published about your business?

> The obvious advantage is free advertising. That's right, if you can create a story that mentions your business in its contents you are getting exposure that is quite often better than if you had purchased an advertisement.

> The next advantage is that people read stories, and do not always read ads. Having your business mentioned in a story increases the chance of connecting with the customer. If your business is mentioned frequently in the newspaper as a supporter of this activity and that, then you are gaining even more exposure through repetition in the public's mind.

How does one get a story written about them in the newspaper?

The best way to do this is to create the story. Creating the story is as simple as it sounds. It is based on the idea that newspapers are always looking for content, especially community oriented papers. If you want a story published, the easiest way is to write it yourself and submit it as a press release.

Let's examine the key points to this process:

1. Create an idea for a story. Good story ideas follow a particular format of interest for a newspaper. The best way to get ideas for your first story is to read the newspaper and see what types of community stories they are publishing. They usually consist of one or more of the following subject matters:

- People doing things to improve the community

- People helping children

- People helping animals

- A community event

- People helping the elderly

- People raising money for charity

- People donating money

- People helping a charity

- Artistic happenings or events

- New businesses opening

- Anything unusual or odd

- Stopping harm on someone, some group or the environment

- Raising awareness on health matters

- People helping some groups considered less fortunate in any category

- People volunteering

- Babies being born

- Couples getting married

- Obituaries

- Sports and competitions

- Current events

- Newly published authors

- Stories with good visualization

- Anything with broad appeal

- Celebrity Tie-in's

- People receiving awards

- People completing certifications, designations or degrees

- Special achievements or recognitions

2. Work out the staging of the story, take photos and write the story into a press release. Make sure the press release is no more than a single page. News paper editors tend to dislike long press releases, and will ignore them. Write concise, but clear and try to tie in one more of the story themes listed above in your press release.

Here is an example:

"John's Automotive in Decatur has had the unprecedented achievement of having three of their mechanics certified in Automobile Brake Repair Systems by the United Auto Training Center in Chicago this month. George Wallace, Roger Clark and Jean Ashgate are all graduates of this rigorous certification course

in auto safety that took several months of intensive hands on training to complete.

On honor of this unprecedented achievement, John Smith owner of John's Automotive has launched a campaign to help children in road safety month in the month of August as recognized by the National Auto Safety Awareness campaign as part of the State of Illinois Department of Transportation. For every person who brings their vehicle in for a brake inspection or repair within the month of August, John's Automotive will donate $10 to the Decatur Children's Emergency Relief Fund as part of the Decatur Children's hospital to offset medical costs and improve care for children involve in auto accidents.

'The Children's Emergency Relief Fund is an important resource within our community, and saves hundreds of children each year' says Mr. Smith 'We will be contributing $10 per person regardless of whether they pay for any repairs or improvements. Our mechanics want to help children who are victims of auto accidents as road safety is important to them.'

To take part in this month long event, visit John's Automotive at 123 Lincoln Hwy in Duluth. To donate directly to the Children's Emergency Relief Fund, call 1-800-896-9111."

Then include a photo of all three mechanics standing in front of the company sign (which hopefully show the phone number in it) holding their completion certificates. Include some children in the photo holding a donation fishbowl of some sort too.

Examine the above story for a moment. Do you see how the various points of interest are worked into the press release to make this interesting to an editor?

The above story has the following worked into it to make it an interesting story to the editors:

- People Achieving Certifications

- People helping children

- People helping a charity

- People preventing harm to others

- People donating money

- It ties in with current events (National Auto Safety Month)

- For the small business marketer, it does the following for the business:

- Subtly mentions how expertly trained and certified your mechanics are.

- It positions the owner and mechanics as concerned citizens that care about children.

- It invites people to come in for a brake inspection with no obligation.

- If the newspaper also publishes the address, it serves as free publicity.

3. The next step once you have the press release written and photo or photos prepared, you will need to get it to the news paper. You will want to find out who the editor is in charge of that section of the newspaper. With smaller newspapers, it is usually best to just call and ask *"If we wanted to submit a story for possible publication, who should we send it to?"*

Once they tell you, ask how they prefer to have it sent over.

Some may want it hand delivered, others will want a fax. More commonly these days they will want it emailed to the story editor over that section with a specific keyword written into the subject line.

Get that information for your first story and then save it for future ones. Verify this information is accurate periodically, as editors tend to shift around within small papers quite frequently. (This too can be a great advantage, as the new editor will likely consider your stories fresh if you frequently send in news articles).

4. Look for other small newspapers that cover your area, and submit the press release to them as well. It is advisable that you change or re-word the content with each individual newspaper submission, even if slightly as quite often small newspaper editors will publish exactly what you submit and it this runs in two separate papers it will not appear like the story is being covered by the newspaper. You want the story to appear like your business just held this event and the newspaper got wind of it, and came to do the story. In reality that seldom happens, but you want the reading audience to perceive it that way.

You will be surprised how often you run into people who saw two or more of the stories about your company in the newspaper, which makes it wise to make sure the stories look slightly different. It is also advisable to submit slightly different photos to each newspaper along with the different written copy which further helps with the illusion of multiple newspapers coming to cover the story about your business. It makes your company appear more like a happening event in the community that way, rather than a shameless promoter.

Another important reason to vary the story and photograph in your press release is that newspaper editors sometimes check up on what the other newspapers are doing.

You will want to have your story look different, or they could get offended and either not publish your story the next time, or edit your content viciously if they do carry the stories in the future. I have also seen them drop out the photo and just carry an abbreviated text of the event, which does not capture as much attention to a reader as one with a photo included in it.

So the lesson here is to vary the press release and photos between each paper you submit it to if submitting the same story to multiple papers.

Some Final Advice

Some final pieces of advice on submitting your own stories to newspapers:

- Grab their attention with a headline in your press release. Make sure it captures their attention and does not let them go.

- Keep your press release to one page or less. Being verbose will quite often get your story ignored. Say enough, but do not say too much.

- Do not submit your press release with typos or grammatical errors. This too can get your story trashed, or worse they will run it as written and make you look bad.

- Editors tend to not like follow up calls to see if the story was received or not. Make sure you have the right submission requirements and follow them.

- If a newspaper decides not to run your story, do not

pester them about it. Just create a new one and move on. Or better yet, send it to another newspaper.

- Makes friends with the media people you work with. These relationships can help you in the long run.

- Make sure you include a contract name, phone numbers and email in all of your press releases. They quite often will call for more information, an interview or just verifying that you did indeed submit the story. Sometimes they will want to send their own photographer for the photos. Make yourself available. It is also a good idea to have a second point of contact included as well as a backup, should your marketing person not be able to be reached. Make sure whoever is the point of contact is well versed with giving interviews. Have a few sound bites on the event that they can say to give more color to the story because the reporters love to quote people in an article.

- Make sure the fun factor is included whenever you do this. Once you have had your first success with a published story, it becomes easier and it is fun to get creative on the next one. In the end it is a great way to promote your business at a local level.

- Additionally, never buy into the idea that once you have done a story that the newspaper will not cover you for a while. I have never found this to be the case. If the story is interesting enough, they will cover it. If you get your creative juices flowing it is possible to get news stories happening at least once a month per newspaper.

Some newspapers will be more challenging than others to get a story into. Do not lose heart, just keep doing it and you will get repeated coverage. Some will only carry one story a year, others once a quarter. Stay on them anyways as editor's change and so do the rules.

I have included some examples of stories I ran for my small company in the 1990's. You can see from some of the dates that there was quite a bit of frequency of our company in the newspaper.

Example #1

Here is an example of a news article that we created from sending a press release about retail stores in our area stocking up for the 1996 Olympics. We tied our store and the story into a local event (the forthcoming Olympics), and received a visit from an Atlanta Journal & Constitution reporter who stopped by the showroom and the result was this article with a full color photo of the products on our showroom floor. This article ran on July 4th, 1996.

THE TOURIST TRADE

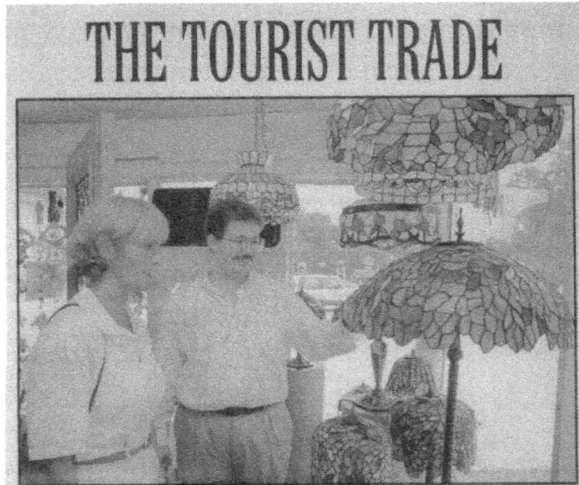

STEVE DEAL / Staff

House of glass: Mike Delaware, owner of Artistic Glass in Roswell, shows Jody Thomas of Dunwoody an array of Tiffany-style lamps. The shop will stay open later during the Games.

Shop owners gearing wares, hours to Olympic visitors

By Chris McDermott
STAFF WRITER

With the Olympics just weeks away and the Historic Roswell Festival coming to town, business people in Roswell are expecting to put in long hours to take advantage of what may be a bonanza.

Mike Delaware owns Artistic Glass on Alpharetta Street, where he sells such items as residential stained and beveled glass windows and doors and Tiffany lamps.

"I'm preparing for an increase in walk-in retail traffic on the smaller items," he said. "We've been stocking up on small lamps, Christmas ornaments, jewelry, porcelain and glass items."

To handle increased business, Delaware said, he's going to be bringing in staff from his production facility and extending his hours, planning to be open from about 11 a.m. to 11 p.m. He's also setting up a tent in back of his store where he'll have live piano music and refreshments.

"We're hoping we'll get a lot of international interest in our work. During the summertime we get a lot of tourists from other states who come in and place orders, so I'm really expecting an increase in the out-of-state orders, and

probably more of a decrease in the local orders, because most of the people's interest here will be downtown."

Acknowledging that there are some businesses that might not draw a lot of tourists, he said, "I've run into some people who are teetering on the edge of whether to stay open at all."

One such person is David Bourne, owner of Photography By David on Green Street.

"For all practical purposes we'll be shut down," Bourne said. "But we look at it not as a bother, but as a fantastic thing that's coming here. While it will impact our business and we will have to make it up at a later time, it is doable."

Bourne said that summers are his busiest time of the year, when he typically photographs about 700 high school seniors.

But for every retailer who may not cash in, there seem to be several more exuding optimism.

Ed Gilliam and his wife, Sandy, run American Sampler, a folk art and craft store on Canton Street, which will be extending its closing time from 5 p.m. to 10 p.m.

"We've heard that Asians especially like crafts made in the United States," said Ed Gilliam. "We think our sales will increase substantially, and we've increased the inventory."

Example #2

This article was a result of a press release after I went to the City of Roswell Mayor and asked him to sign a proclamation declaring it 'Louis Comfort Tiffany Day' in Roswell on February 18th, 1997. We hosted a special event and invited people from the community. This was an event entirely created on a short notice. We looked up Tiffany's birthday and decided it would be an event in our store. The Mayoral proclamation helped to get us the coverage in the newspaper, and then we staged the photograph to feature our lamps and our top sales woman.

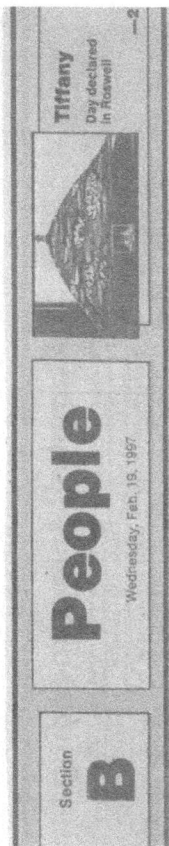

Pictured is stained glass designer Amanda Skinner preparing the display of Tiffany Lamps at Artistic Glass. Artistic Glass boasts a wide selection of stained glass and Tiffany Lamps. Artistic Glass will host a ceremony denoting Feb. 18 as Louis Comfort Tiffany Day in the City of Roswell.

Tiffany Day declared by City of Roswell

By Ingram Thornton
North Fulton Neighbor Staff Writer

In celebration of the birth and life of Louis Comfort Tiffany, the City of Roswell and the artists at Artistic Glass are declaring February 18th Louis Comfort Tiffany Day in the City of Roswell.

On Tuesday, Feb. 18, the first annual Gala celebration will be held from 7- 9 p.m. in Tiffany's honor at Artistic Glass, 242 Alpharetta St. in Roswell. The ceremony will include a long awaited dedication of an original window to Louis Comfort Tiffany, designed and created by the award winning artists at Artistic Glass. In addition there will be a magnificent original Tiffany lamp present for viewing, valued at $25,000.

Louis Comfort Tiffany was born on Feb. 18, 1848, as the son of the wealthy Charles Tiffany, founder of Tiffany & Co. Jewelers, New York. Not wishing to join the family business and with an understanding of his father's approval, he began to study art and ultimately created a new art form.

After two years of study with the great American painter George Inness, he went abroad to England, France and North America for further study. In England he was fascinated by the 'Beaux Arts' movement where

one artist would create paintings, vases, wall paper and other items of decor. Like other artists of the period, he took on the expanded role of interior decorator. However, in France he was totally overwhelmed by the beauty of the stained glass windows and ceilings. This was the turning point for the future of stained glass arts worldwide.

Through painstaking research he developed and patented the technique for manufacturing opalescent glass and favrile glass. He is also responsible for the development of the "Copper-foil" techniques that are still broadly used in the craft of stained glass today.

As his fame grew, he was commissioned to do windows and ceilings for the White House, the Presidential Palace in Cuba and the homes of America's wealthiest families. While working with Thomas Edison on lighting the first movie theater, the Lyceum, Edison suggested to Tiffany that he also make table lamps. Within a few years, the lamps of Tiffany Studios became the rage in the United States and Europe.

Today Tiffany lamps are sought by collectors. One such lamp, the Magnolia, sold for $528,000 in 1985, confirming Tiffany as the most expensive form of Art Nouveau.

Example #3

Here is another news story that we created from a press release we sent in on our stores participation in an upcoming home show. The newspaper wanted to use our stained glass as the central color photo in the article. Once again we featured our products and our sales people in the shot. This article ran on September 10th, 1997 and it ran on the front page of the Neighbor section.

Street of Dreams

North Fulton residents will be joined by visitors from all around the metro area in touring the 1997 Street of Dreams. The tour started Aug. 23, and already the event is expecting record-breaking crowds. Located in the Hamilton Mill subdivision, the show features not only homes and lawns, but featured designers as well. Pictured from left are Alpharetta residents Amanda Skinner, head designer for Artistic Glass in Roswell and Kevin Rice, decorative glass designer. Ms. Skinner designed the window in the background.

Beautiful lawns and homes await on the Street

By Cassandra A. Brimmer
North Fulton Neighbor Staff Writer

The Hamilton Mill subdivision in neighboring Gwinnett County is the host of the seventh "Street of Dreams" tour, featuring five new luxury homes fully decorated, designed, and custom built for the public to view or purchase unique homes filled with a multitude of design applications and innovative ideas.

This year's tour, a five-week festival, is set to be one of the largest in crowd expectancy. Labor Day weekend drew a record crowd since the tour

Up close

■ **What:** Street of Dreams.

■ **When:** Aug. 23 through Sept. 28, 10 a.m. to 8 p.m. Tuesday through Sunday, closed Mondays.

■ **Admission:** $6 for Adults, $7 for children 4-12 years and senior citizens.

■ **How:** For information call (404) 914-1350.

opened on Aug. 23rd. The show will run through Sept. 28th. This year the tour is expecting

crowds approaching 60,000 visitors.

"Everything is accessible," said Sharon Goldmacher, president of Communications 21.

Visitors will have access to everything the $4,100 to $8,140 square-foot homes has to offer. The homes are for sale and are valued at $470,000 to $580,000. The furniture, window treatments and tons of accessories are available for sale at a discounted rate.

Each home is very diverse in design, colors and decorations. Presentations will be done by five of Atlanta's top-rated builders, interior designers, architects, furniture galleries, landscapers and suppliers. Vis-

itors will also have a chance to vote on the homes they like best.

"7,000 people toured this one house," said Phil Voss, showroom manager of Artistic Glass. Voss has participated in the tour for 20 years, he will have a display of beveled glass doors, antique glass and stained glass windows. "This is open to all people," he said.

The show hours are 10 a.m. to 8 p.m. Tuesday through Sunday, closed on Mondays. Admission price for adults is $6, senior citizens and children 4-12 years old is $7. Admission is free for children 3 years old and younger. For more information please call (770) 914-7961.

Example #4

Here is another example of a story our showroom created from a press release we sent to the Atlanta Business Chronicle. They sent a reporter out and he wrote and published this story. This newspaper was a challenging one to get into, but we persisted sending press release ideas over several months and finally got them to cover our store. This article ran on October 2, 1998.

AROUND THE REGION

High-end home stores flourish in Roswell

NORTH FULTON — Artistic Glass will have its day on Oct. 3. The Roswell City Council has proclaimed that Saturday Artistic Glass Day, in honor of the city's 15-year-old store. Artistic Glass, situated north of the city's square, specializes in custom-stained and beveled glass doors and windows. It targets individual homeowners interested in high-

facility in Alpharetta, which also honored the store for its 15th anniversary.

The owner of Artistic Glass, Michael Delaware, was cited for his continued community involvement. Delaware has been president of the Roswell Merchants Association for five years, and he is the retail representative to the Historic Roswell Convention and Visitors Bureau.

"The thing I've learned about the average businessman is, they tend to bury their head in their business," Delaware said. "And when the steamroller of politics comes by, they get rolled over."

Delaware helped his sister and brother-in-law start the business in 1983, and along with two partners, purchased it from them six years ago. The company now has 25 employees and is growing. Delaware said that Artistic Glass surpassed last year's sales in August of this year.

Having its day: Roswell Mayor Jere Wood (second from right) stands with Bill Simpson (left), Michael Delaware and Betty Adkins, all of Artistic Glass.

end glass with aesthetic appeal.

In addition to the showroom in Roswell, Artistic Glass has a production

Courtesy of the Atlanta Business Chronicle Oct 1998

Example #5

Here is a story that we created with another press release. This was the result of another press release we sent to about our studio's participation in an upcoming home show. We simply repeated the tactic we used in the prior year, and there were new editors and reporters by the time this show came around again and we repeated the same high profile article on the front page of the Neighbors Section. This article ran on September 30, 1998.

Street of Dreams

From left: Stacy Johnson, a Roswell decorative glass designer, and Michael Delaware, president of Artistic Glass. Delaware designed the glass on the door, which features a pineapple—the international symbol of hospitality. The Street of Dreams at White Columns runs until Nov. 8.

White Columns hosts 1998's home show event

Example #6

Finally here was an article that our store ran about our showroom having won an award at the Atlanta Festival of Trees. We had created a stained glass Christmas tree for the entry in coordination with the Radio station we were advertising on, and won the 'Best in Show' award for the unique design. We used this award to send out several press releases and the result was over seven separate articles in different newspapers covering the story. Here is an example of one of the stories that ran in the Roswell Neighbor on December 18, 1996.

Small photo by F.C. Palm

Festival has local winners

A stained glass tree constructed by Artistic Glass of Roswell won first place for the Chairman's Award at the Egleston Children's Hospital Festival of Trees. The tree was on display at the festival. Holding the commemorative plaque are, from left, Phil Voss, of Roswell, showroom manager at Artistic Glass; Michael Delaware, of Woodstock, president of Artistic Glass; and Bill Simpson, of East Cobb, an owner of Artistic Glass. The tree was designed by Delaware, Simpson and Mark Webb.

Printed with permission of the Roswell Neighbor
Dec 18, 1996 (Photo F.C. Palm)

Direct Mail

As the world goes into more and more of a digital age it is easy to forget about direct mail as a marketing tool. In comparison to sending out messages to identities electronically, direct mail it far more expensive.

However, it can still be far more successful for many types of businesses than any other medium. If you are in the business of selling anything related to the home, for example, one should strongly consider the use of direct mail. As long as people receive mail at their home, direct mail can be an effective and valuable marketing tool.

However, due to the fact that costs can add up as one is attempting to reach more people, it is essential to know some basics that apply to this. As the world goes faster and faster, it further becomes important to know some basics on what works and what does not work in the world of direct mail if one is going to maximize the potential of this marketing tool. To ignore these basics, one can waste a lot of money doing the wrong moves.

To begin, here are three basic rules of Direct Mail advertising to keep it simple. There is a great deal to be learned on this subject alone, but following these three guidelines will allow you to focus on what is important.

Rule One - Consider that all forms of Direct Mail are merely *3 second advertising*. What this means is from the moment a person handles the mail in their mail box, and in fact looks through it to sort it, you have 3 seconds for your piece to get consideration. The consideration that recipient is determining most often is *'Trash or Keep'*. You have 3 seconds to convince them your piece of unsolicited mail is a keeper, and does not deserve the trash can. What this means it that your message needs to impress and communicate or it will be tossed.

Rule Two: Direct Mail should be readable, simple rather than verbose in terms of copy and capture the attention of the audience and deliver your message to them.

Rule Three: Direct Mail if more effective when one mails three pieces over time to a smaller mailing list, rather than a onetime mailing to a large mailing list. Repetitive and frequent mailings are more successful than singular or less frequent mailings.

Writing Good Copy

How does one write good copy for a direct mail piece? Before one can write copy for any form of written or printed advertising, one should know the answers to these questions on this checklist:

- What is the target audience one is trying to reach?

- What is the product or service one is trying to sell?

- What are all the product or service benefits?

- What are all the features of the product or service?

- How is this product or service different from the competition?

- How much can the buyer reasonably expect to pay?

- Will the product or service be purchased for business or personal use?

- What would be the logical follow up product or service to sell them after they have purchased this one?

- Will you need to show the product is color to communicate it properly?

- Are you offering a payment plan or financing option?

- Will the product or service be a good gift item?

- Does the product require a detailed description or a simple one?

- What are the most salient points about the product or service that the customer needs to know to retain it in memory or prompt them into action?

- Do you need photos or illustrations in the direct mail piece to communicate the product or service?

- Can you use 'before' and 'after' pictures to sell this product or service?

- Can you tie the copy into some current event or news story?

- Should you consider a celebrity endorsement?

- Does the product sell better in a particular region?

- Is the product or service seasonal, and does it sell better in a particular climate?

- What must you include in the copy to give the prospective buyer a sense of urgency to buy it?

- Can you use scientific evidence or statistical data to prove the effectiveness of your product or service?

Finding Mailing Lists

Once you have established what your market audience is and what you are going to say, promote, etc. Where do you obtain the mailing lists to send it to?

There are a lot of online resources these days for acquiring mailing lists. One of the more established and long term companies is Haines & Company which produces the *Criss Cross Directory*. Their website is: ***www.criss-cross.com***

This type of directory groups addresses by streets as opposed to just cities. This is useful if you have a product for example that is only going to appeal to a home owner. It allows you to select specific streets and target a geographic area. Let's assume you sell a premium garage door system. With such a product, you are going to more successful with homes that have a garage than ones that do not. Larger homes will have a two and three car garage.

With broad mailing lists that you buy for a zip code, you are given everything in the zip code that is residential, which can often include apartment complexes and duplexes. If you are selling a garage door, this is the wrong target audience. *Criss Cross* directories give you the freedom to research your market area and individually mail to this streets and target neighborhoods.

If one is uncertain about what are the better target neighborhoods, one can always consult with the field sales team. They will be able to help you narrow down the neighborhoods that are likely to buy the product you are promoting. One can also simply target neighborhoods of past buyers.

One of the best secrets about using Criss Cross is to use this system to precisely target the neighbors of people that have recently bought your product. With the magic of computer software and digital photography, one can go so far as to snap a photo of that recently installed garage door system at 123 Cherry Lane and produce a small quantity of say 50 post cards with an image of the installation, the address and a message saying something like *"We recently installed the XYZ Superior Garage door system at 123 Cherry Lane..."* Then mail it to all the homes on the street and cross streets. Curious neighbors will drive by and look, and this is a great way to sell other jobs on the same street.

I once used this marketing approach with a beveled glass door company I owned in Atlanta. The results were outstanding. Due to the fact that the printing quantity was so small, the cost was a little more per piece.

However, the advantage is that we had a secretary take these postcards and hand address them with a personal hand-written note, and then mailed them. The results were incredible. It became a form of micro-targeted marketing, allowing us to cut out the cost in our marketing budget and maximize our effectiveness. It was not uncommon for us to sell seven or eight homes on a specific street in using this campaign, as the more neighbors who purchased the more jumped on to upgrade their home.

There are also companies that offer mailing lists to target specific professions and demographics. This can be incredibly effective for the right product. Buying a list of dentists in a region when you are selling a new X-Ray system or medical waste disposal system would be one example.

A few examples of such companies include:

Info USA: www.infousa.com

Unlimited Mailing Lists: *www.infofree.com*

Direct Mail: www.directmail.com

These companies charge for the lists, and send them to you in some format. An important thing to try to negotiate with these companies is the ability to use the list multiple times without having to pay for each successive mailing or use of the same list. There are many such companies out there that are offering mailing lists. Just go to any search engine and search 'Mailing Lists' or 'USPS mailing lists' and start doing research.

As a small business marketing strategy, it is better to mail repeated times to a small list rather than one time to a large list. So try to obtain mailing lists that allow you repeated or unlimited use to specified target audiences.

Here are three important qualities of a perfect mailing list:

> ➢ One that allows multiple or unlimited use.

> ➢ One that can demonstrate current up-to-date information (You do not want to use a list that results in large amount of return mail because the data is too outdated).

> ➢ One that allows you to target a specific audience by category and geographic location as needed.

What are some of the categories of audiences can you purchase as mailing listings? Every company you purchase from will have different categories, so be sure to explore what is available. Here is a list of some of the categories that are commonly available in mailing lists from these online companies:

- Age groups

- Married or Single
- Gender
- Home Value
- Estimated Household Income
- Ethnicity
- Households by Religious Affiliation
- Households with Children
- Hobbies & Interests
- Homeowners
- Apartment Renters
- Pet Owners
- Wealthy Americans
- Millionaires
- Casino Gamblers
- Magazine Readers
- Stocks & Bond Investors
- Diet & Weight Loss Groups
- Real Estate Investors
- Golfers
- Cruise Travelers

- Runners & Joggers

- Camping & Hiking

- Boat Owners

- Attorneys

- Accountants & CPA's

- Real Estate Agents

- Physicians

- Contractors

- Pilots

- Insurance Agents

- Aircraft Owners

- Farmers

- Dentists

- Nurses

- Large businesses

- Small businesses

- Businesses with trucking and fleets

- Restaurants

- Schools & Universities

- Wholesale & Distributors

- Employee Size

- Retail Stores

- Annual Sales Volume of a Business

- Industry Specific

- Trade Show Attendees

- Direct Mail Responders

- Trade Publication Subscribers

- Then there are entire mailing lists in the *'new'* or *'recent'* category, including:

- New homeowners

- New businesses

- New movers

- New parents

- Recently Married

- Recently Divorced

- Business Bankruptcies

- Consumer Bankruptcies

- Business Liens

- Consumer Liens

- Business Judgments

- Consumer Judgments

- Recently Retired

- New Car Owners

The more targeted your mailing list, the greater chance of success from that list. Be willing to experiment. Sometimes surveying your existing customers can offer great insight to their personal interests, and therefore give you a clue to what your target audience for your product or service.

For example, let's say you are running a catering business and you discover that a lot of your clients are golfers through a basic hobby and interest survey of existing clients. This might offer you a clue that sending a direct mail promotion to a mailing list of golfers in your area could create some new customers.

Another example might be finding out from a survey that out of the last 15 customers who bought a specific type of mini-van that 13 were pet owners might offer you a clue to purchase a 'pet owner' mailing list and send out a photo of a dog sitting in the back seat of this new mini-van, etc.

To make direct mail work for a small business, one needs to not only research on the front end, but also have a system in place to measure responses after the mailing has occurred.

A good way to do this is to have the sales people or any personnel who answer the incoming calls to log each caller by date, time and name of when the called, and also their response to the question 'How did you find out about us?' Customers will usually be willing to answer this question, and most are accustomed to it. It is also an indicator to many experienced customers that this is a business that is interested in their own marketing results.

Quite often new small business owners abandon the use of direct mail in favor of other less expensive or cheaper marketing approaches.

Sometimes they get lucky and have success, but many times they fail to properly isolate their target audience and make the mistake of paying for a large mailing list and sending it out one time.

They see the poor response (because they did not find a target audience and took the 'shot gun blast' approach) and they only paid for one mailing, and did not engage in repetition.

The Magic of Repetition in Direct Mail Marketing

I was once the co-owner of a small business in Atlanta metro-area that custom designed, manufactured and installed stained and beveled glass in the home. We had an ongoing marketing system in place where we mailed approximately 300 to 500 hand addressed postcards each week to specific neighborhoods that we circled on the regional map.

I once had a stay at home mom that would sit at her kitchen table and address these postcards for me at 5 cents a card and rotate around the map over a 3 month period using a *Criss Cross* Directory as described earlier. We always sent out a colored post card of the front entryway of one of the homes we installed, and in the copy contained the phone number and the offer for a 'Free in-home estimate'.

With this system in place after the first few months we knew we had a good thing. The phones would ring with an average of 5 to 8 calls each week asking for a free in-home estimate, and the sales people who went were coming home with a 90% closing ratio on all of these appointments. We could almost count on an average of 4 to 5 sales a week from these appointments, and ultimately my salespeople loved to get these calls and go on the appointment because they were good prospects.

As a manager over the area, I sometimes went on these field sales appointments when the sales people could not make it. On one occasion, after we had been doing these mailings for approximately five years, I went to one of these 'free in-home estimate' appointments. I met with the customers, and made the sale on a new front entry door system. Once we had wrapped up the paperwork, the couple asked me to come into the kitchen as they wanted to show me something else. The lady walked over to a kitchen drawer and pulled out a stack of about seven of our postcards that she had collected over the years.

She told me that each time she saw a new picture come in the mail she saved it in hopes of some future date to make this purchase. She had a selection of seven different photos of door entryways that we had mailed to her over the years! This is the best example of the power of repetition marketing that I had ever seen. She told me that it took all of this time for her to call because she was saving up money and trying to convince her husband by constantly pinning our postcards on the refrigerator. She said she had been saving them for about four or five years!

So consider this for a moment. Our company was mailing over and over again to the same neighborhoods over a five year period, changing the photo occasionally on the card. We used repetition Direct Mail and we were generating an average of 4-5 front entry door systems sold per week from this campaign. Each entry system averaged $3000 to $5000 per individual order. Our out of pocket cost per mailing was a budget of $375 per week, or $1500 a month. In essence we were getting back $10 for every $1 we were spending on this marketing campaign by mailing over and over again to the same houses.

Over the years with our business, we tried many other types of marketing and did receive incredible results from a diversified campaign. However, we never abandoned our direct mail campaign in all the years I owned the company. We did adjust it from time to time as we added new neighborhoods, and changed the postcards, but the philosophy of repetitive mailings to our targeted audience was always a constant and a secret of our success.

Types of Mailings for Direct Mail

What types of Direct Mail really work? When one considers that the average consumer often gets mailed to them all forms of what is quite often coined as 'junk mail' it is important to recognize that they are desensitized to Direct Mail marketing. Therefore any piece that you mail must stand out as different and interesting, or your Direct Mail piece which you spent so much time on will find its way into the trash can as they recipient sorts through the mail.

Here are a few tips on how to make specific types of mailers work:

Postcards:

Here are some key points regarding postcards:

- Use a graphic, photo or illustration of some kind on one side that clearly and visually catches the attention of the prospective target buyer. Use your creative imagination to get their attention with minimum word copy.

- Make sure your copy on the reverse side is simple and direct. Include a concise written description of the product or service.

- Include a large type bold phone number complete with area code in the middle of the card. Never make the phone number small if you are trying to prompt a call as a response. Quite often marketing gurus forget that not everyone who receives this mailing will have 20/20 vision, and if there is any information you want them to remember or act upon, it is your phone number.

- Include a website, email, Facebook page any other important contact information related to the internet.

- If including a physical location which you are trying promote like a new store, be sure to also include a small map with a star on it indicating where the location is.

- Avoid unreadable or light colors. Dark colors for the ink work best such as black, brown, red, green or blue. The reason for this is that your prospect may first see this promotional piece at night or in a poorly lit room, and with the '3 Second rule' in consideration as they sort their mail over a garbage can, you want to make sure your copy is clearly readable in whatever lighting situation. For this same reason, avoid dark photographs and backgrounds that might not communicate the imagery or copy in dim lighting.

Once you have found a successful postcard, you might look into printing them in larger quantities to save on cost per piece. If you are using color postcards with color photos, this can be very important to consider. Printing a color photo postcard in quantities of 50,000 to 100,000 at a time can save tremendously in your per piece price. However, you want to make sure that your mailing piece is proven and successful before you take the plunge to pay for that many copies. The virtue of postcards is that they can be printed in larger quantities and take up less storage space than letters, envelopes and newsletters.

Letter or envelopes:

Letters or any kind of envelope one must consider that getting your message across is a two step process that a prospect must engage in during the 3 second window. The prospect will scan it, and if interested must take the second step of opening it.

To get them to move past the 'scan it' step, one can apply and follow many of the tips listed above for a post card. Additionally, one can also include bright colored writing with a short message.

Try also using unusually colored envelopes like bright yellow, green, red or blue. Choose an envelope of a color, shape or design they are not used to seeing.

Another great trick is to include what is known as a 'grabber' inside the envelope. It is usually that small mystery object placed inside that makes a lump and compels them to open it and find out what it is. Go to the dollar store and find tiny rubber eraser heads, toys, jewelry or seed packet or some other thing that you can place in there and create enough of a mystery about what it is to compel them to open it.

Fold over Fliers or Newsletters:

Fold over fliers or newsletters can be effective, however, if created with too thin a paper can get torn or damaged in the mailing process and arrive at the prospects homes looking terrible. So always choose a heavier pound paper such as 30 lb or above for this use, never a 10 lb paper.

Follow the same attention grabbing tips as covered in post cards and letters.

Newsletters work great to keep existing customers returning to your store. They should be personal and interesting, and include useful information. Always include a coupon or incentive to have them come back in and save money.

Also include something on the front that gives tidbits of what it inside. Try to give them a teaser to create interest enough to get them to open it. I once created a newsletter that had a small article about a local radio station DJ's coming to our showroom. As a teaser on the cover we included a 'Inside this issue: *Randy & Spiff get naked (Just kidding!)*' and this turned out to have been the most read newsletter we ever published in accordance with the feedback we received from our customers.

Value Envelope Mailings:

There are mailing companies such as ***www.valpak.com*** that offer the service of paying for a advertisement flyer inside a mailing envelope that they mail to households in an entire zip code. This company has also expanded to other digital mailing advertising products as well in recent years that you can learn about on their website.

These can be very effective for certain companies. The best results seem to be to offer a coupon or *'call for a free in-home estimate'* with a special discount feature. If your company cannot offer such a discount or feature, then it may not work for you.

There is a group of buyers who regularly go through these types of value envelopes whenever they come in. Make sure your advertisement grabs their attention with a photo or graphic of your product, the offer of a discount in big bold letters and your phone number and/or website or it will get tossed into the trash can as they sort through the packet.

Summary of Direct Mail

as a Marketing Tool

Direct mail marketing still today is a niche tool for the small business marketer, and can yield some incredible results if applied with the common sense tips presented in this chapter. It done poorly without taking the necessary steps to find the right message for your target audience, it can become quite costly.

The best advice on using Direct Mail marketing is to experiment on a small scale with a mailing piece, and measure the response. A good piece mailed out in a small quantity of 100 that yields 5 responses will likely yield 50 responses per thousand. This is a good Direct mail piece. If the responses then are continued to be measured to see which ones in fact turn the corner to become a sale, then you will know if you have a *great Direct Mail piece* or not.

A great Direct Mail piece pulls in the target audience and *creates sales*. Remember that point always. One can easily fall prey to the illusion that one has a great piece simply because people respond to it, but if the response you are getting does not result in sales, then one of two things needs to change:

1. The Direct Mail piece needs adjustment.

2. The people handling the calls need a new pitch or additional training to turn these leads into sales.

It takes some time to really measure the results of a Direct Mail campaign. It is not done in a few days or a single week. It quite often takes several weeks or sometimes months to see if it is bringing about results. This will quite often depend on the typical length of your sales process.

With some products, it takes prospective buyers longer to make a decision whereas with other products they are an impulse buy, and the customers are driven into a store or location. In such a case as the latter, if marketing surveys after sales in the store are indicating that people are walking in because of the Direct Mail piece and buying, then you have a great mailing piece on your hands.

Once you have a successful Direct Mailing piece, continue to use it and other slight variations of it as a regular campaign. Continue without changing your approach until the Direct Mail piece starts to not generate a response then adjust it or try a new one. One can also place this great piece on a rotational mailing schedule with other Direct mail pieces and use it in a repetition campaign on a target area.

One should always realize that a Direct Mail piece may be a seasonal piece, even though it may not appear upon face value to be one. It may tend to get a particular high response during a specific season of the year that you mail it. Sometimes this does not become clear until later when you measure the results.

For example, I had one particular Direct Mail piece that always pulled 3X the response when mailed in November and December, and the only difference from the other cards we mailed was that it had a reddish background and red border, and it seemed to tie in with the holidays in the minds of the consumer. When we mailed any other piece during that time, it did not pull as much response. Likewise, when we mailed that reddish colored piece at other times of the year, it pulled like any of the other normal pieces. So without realizing it we had created a successful seasonal Direct Mailing postcard.

Overall Direct Mail will always be a good marketing tool as long as people still receive mail at home or at the office. Until there is some radical change in the way mail is delivered, it warrants investigation for use by the small business marketer.

As a final note, when creating a direct mail piece, consider other advertisers who might also want to have their product featured on a small portion of the mailer. If they are willing to cover some of the cost, this can be another form of use for 'cooperative advertising' to offset printing costs. If you explore this as a possibility, you might be surprised at what other products might want to share in the expense.

I once had Weiser Locks pay for a 70% of my printing costs on 50,000 postcards simply by featuring their logo and a lockset the custom door featured inset into the photograph that I was marketing. Cooperative advertising can be a great way to reduce costs, and it can be a win-win situation for both advertisers.

The Business Card

The business card is quite often the one item many small business marketers overlook in terms of their value. So in this chapter we are going to examine two very important aspects of the business card: The *content* and *their use*.

The Content

Let's look at the content of a business card. What is the most important information you need on a business card? Here is a list of some of the common information found on business cards:

- Your name

- Your Title, Job or Position

- Description of the services you offer

- Your company name

- Your phone number(s)

- Your mailing address

- Your email

- Your website or blog

- Your Facebook address

- Your Twitter handle

- Other social media contact info

- Company logo

- Photos

- Graphics

- Color

- Messages, tag lines or catch phrases

So of all of this information listed above, which is the most important? In days prior to the internet this was very easy to define, yet even then it was overlooked by many small business owners. The most important information in the pre-internet age was 'What your company is about' and your phone number. Your name and company name were secondary to the client getting the message on '*what you are all about*' and having access to your *phone number*.

On a business card, how can you design it for the phone number to be easily found above all the other information you provide? Here are some suggestions:

- Make it bold text and larger than the other type on the card

- Place it in the center of the card or some other unique position that catches the attention of the person who looks at it.

- Consider making it in a different color from the rest of the text such as red, blue or a dark green.

- Take some time today and collect up some business cards people have given to you over the years. Which ones can you easily see the phone number on? Which ones have a readable phone number? You might be surprised to find that many business cards place contact information including the phone number in small type at the bottom or side, and sometimes on the back, and make the logo or some other image of message more visible.

There is truth in the information that you want the recipient of the card to know what your company is about as mentioned above, but it is not always communicated first through a logo. It can often be a graphic showing what you do or sometimes just the description of what you do.

So when a person sees your business card, you want two things to happen:

1) You want them to instantly see what you do and how to

contact you.

2) You want them to be interested enough to feel there is value is keeping your card.

In today's internet age other important information that people will be looking for is your website, blog or **Facebook** contact information. Email is also important, but most of the time people are looking for a website to find out more on '*what you are all about*'.

So making this information visible and readable is also important. In designing a business card is essential. Factoring in design to make it interesting and appealing is necessary also to achieve that design for someone to retain the card for future use.

The Use of the Business Card

Business cards have a magical way of circulating around sometimes. The only way this can happen however is for the card to be placed in every possible location one can find. So often business card use gets allocated to handing it to clients and customers that walk into your place of business or the ones you interact with. This is important in their use for that future contact; however, there is another use that is quite often neglected.

The neglected form of use for a business card is the application of dissemination everywhere you go. Remember the children's tale of Johnny Appleseed? Where reportedly Johnny Appleseed walked the countryside tossing apple seeds around in an effort to promote the growth of apples all over the country? Not every tree of course grew, but he tossed around enough of them as legend has it that apples became a common crop all over the country. The use of the business card in promotion has a similar application. In order for business to grow from it, it must be planted in every place possible. Not every place you plant it will result in someone buying from you, but you never know where that card will end up.

Business cards are the cheapest form of printing that one can invest in for printed promotion. They have been around a very long time, and even in the age of the internet, they will likely continue for years to come as one of the remaining forms of promotion of professional contact information. The mindset one needs to get into is to use the business card as a tool to reach people you have never met before, as well as people you casually meet.

The way you do this is to always have your business card with you and leave it everywhere you go. If you have a small business that appeals to the broad public and prospects come from all walks of life, leave your card everywhere. If you go to a restaurant, leave one with the tip. If you go to the store to buy something, leave one with the clerk who checks you out.

If you have perhaps a narrower public for your business, you can still leave your card everywhere because you never know when you card may get passed along to the right person who is your customer. Business cards can also be inserted inside any outgoing mail you have, including your bills.

I once came across a man who sold cars and stamped his business card information on the backs of all of his outgoing checks. The idea was that every check passes through the hands of many different clerks along the way, and periodically he got calls back. He even went so far as to place a second stamp on his check after he sent the first one out with his card information that read *"To date I have paid your company _____ dollars for your services. How about sending me a referral or two to help my business?"* He would then write in the amount on the blank line.

Placing your business card information in front of as many people as you can is a basic strategy that has to be a part of any small business marketing plan. Those cards do no good sitting idle on your desk. They are far more useful in the hands of a prospective customer. Get them out there everywhere.

Another story that might interest you is a Realtor I know who started brand new to the business in 2002. He did not know where to find prospects when he first began, so he went and stood in front of a popular convenience store near some neighborhoods he wanted to sell houses in.

He greeted every person he saw coming into the store and gave him a business card saying *"Hi my name is Steve I am a Realtor in the area. I help people buy and sell houses. Pleased to meet you. Do you or anyone you know need some help with selling or finding a home? Here is my card..."* and then shook their hand and handed them a business card. It helped him meet people and start some conversations. He even developed a few leads. He did this for a few hours every day, and it got his phone starting to ring and his business was started all from getting his business card out there.

When looking at your business card, ask yourself the following:

- If a new person who knew nothing about your business saw this for the first time, would it communicate what product or service you offer and clearly how to reach you?

- Is it simple, yet readable?

- Is it something that you would want to hold onto for possible future use?

- Can people easily find you if they found your card lying around?

- Finally, do people call you from this card when you hand it out?

These points are very basic, but they are the fundamental important aspects of *business card design, creation* and *practical use.* If your card can pass the above five points with a resounding 'Yes' then you probably have a good card. Use it broadly and you will see positive results. It is better than them sitting in a drawer.

The Power of the Internet

When one considers the global size and scope of the internet today, it is almost humorous to look back to quotes from the early 1990's in the early stages of its development:

"The Internet is becoming a hotbed of commercial activity and advertising. A dozen firms are creating `electronic malls' and other `places' on the Web to draw potential shoppers en masse." (Business Week, Nov 1994)

"Hot technologies such as on-line information services and new computer programs can garner you millions more in revenues. ... With a worldwide audience of millions, the Internet has the power to transform a local company into a global entity instantaneously." (Success, June 1995)

"The Internet has produced at least one very tangible benefit: Seemingly, every organization in the real universe is represented in this ethereal one. Many government agencies, research centers, universities, corporations, and media outlets are there now, and the rest are on the way. The wondrous power of the Internet has

been unleashed by the new electronic network known as the World Wide Web." (New York Times, Mar 19, 1995)

Without a doubt, the internet has evolved far beyond the expectations and dreams envisioned in 1995. Not even on the radar back or predicted was the rise in popularity of social media and how it has come to influence all forms of people's lives and the world of business.

For the small business marketer, there is always something new and exciting to explore and discover as a resource on the internet. The following chapters will tap into some of the basic foundation of tools for any small business marketing campaign. These should be considered and explored for use in reaching out for our ever changing customer base in this new and exciting computerized world we live in.

Websites & Blogging

When one thinks of an online presence, most small business owners think of getting a website. Websites are essential in this information age as it gives a customer a chance to find out about your business from the comforts of their own home without having to call. They can also do business with your company online if you have e-commerce set up. However, when almost every business has a website, how does one draw attention to your company's website online for it to generate business for the company? How does one get their message to rise up above all the noise of the competition?

To answer this one must first understand the difference between a *website* and a *blog*. It is perhaps easier to understand their functions first:

A website: This is a stationary place to do business.

A blog: This is a *dynamic changing tool* to share information and refer back to the website.

With a website one can provide all the information to contact the company, email, submit a request form, watch video, read information about the company, products and services, etc. They can also purchase products, set appointments and many other functions that you build into the site to make it more user friendly. It is a stationary place much like a storefront where people can visit it in the real world, except it is online.

A blog is a dynamic or changing entity. It consists of new articles, photos and information being posted on a regular basis. Blogs get more search engine notice because they are considered current information on a subject. Google for example structures most of their searching algorithms to seek out what they refer to as '*dynamic content*'.

Dynamic content is the bread and butter of blogs. The content changes, and updates, etc. That is why when you search a news story on a particular subject matter on Google, you most often get a blog article posted that day or in recent history over a website that posts information about the same subject matter.

Both websites and blogs have an important role for the small business marketer. The website becomes your store front, and the blog becomes your road sign pointing to the store front. Keeping a blog with new and changing content related to your products and services can take some creativity, but the more you do it the more you will find it becomes easier and easier.

As an example, if a small business was a flower shop they might take the following approach for their website and blog. Set up a website that allows people to read about your products, place an order and pay right there at the website. Then to draw attention to the website, create a blog or two that writes stories about flowers in people's lives. You can even write articles about types of flowers and what they mean when you give them for what occasion, etc. Position your blog as the *flower expert* within your community, and always direct people to your website to 'find out more'. The small business marketer could also post these blog articles on Facebook and send them out on Twitter, etc.

One does not always have to hire a professional to set up a blog or website. One can find out a lot of useful information about how to set one up for free by simply watching YouTube videos on the subject. There is a lot to learn about blogging and building a website, but if your role for your company is marketing then it should be something you consider doing yourself if you can find the time.

One can also hire someone to help you set up a website or blog and teach you to update it yourself, etc. That way you are paying for a onetime fee for set up and then updating and making changes on your own. There are many products and services available online to build one's own website and blog.

Here are a few places you can start:

www.wordpress.com

www.webs.com

www.webstarts.com

Most blogs are either based on the Wordpress format or the Blogger format. When you build your own blog through Wordpress, you should also weigh the differences between using *Wordpress.com* and *Wordpress.org*.

Wordpress.com = Allows you to build your blogs for

free, but you cannot sell or 'monetize' this type of blog.

Wordpress.org = Allows you to monetize the blog, but requires that you self-host the blog through a separate hosting service such as *www.godaddy.com* or *www.hostgator.com*.

Monetizing your blog will allow you to sell your products and make money with them as if people click on your ads, make purchases from your ads, etc.

Blogger.com is also a free blog creating service that is part of Google. You can monetize these blogs through Google as well.

If you want to find out about monetizing your blog and website, I recommend that you look for self-help videos on YouTube to find out up to date ways to do this. There are a lot of great tutorials that will walk you through it step by step, and Google has some as well.

So from a small business marketer's perspective, it is best to consider websites as stationary places to arrive at and blogs as the ever-changing road sign pointing the way to the website. The blog therefore could be thought of that billboard that pops up when one is cruising through the information super highway, and gives the viewer some information they are looking for and then redirects them off the highway to the main storefront or in this case a website. If you can think within that simple framework, you will have the basic understanding of how and why you need a website and blog.

How often should you write to a blog? The really active ones that get the most attention are updated 2-3 times a day. However, the average business person does not have time for that. The advantages of using Wordpress, however, allows you to write blog articles in advance and schedule them out to be posted in the future. The best starting out strategy is to write a blog post to cover at least once a month at first, and schedule it out in advance. Then increase it to once a week, then twice a week, and so forth. You will find that once you see response from your blog articles that it becomes easier to write more.

One can also have as many blogs as you want. The topics can vary slightly, and perhaps address different aspects of your products and services. Each unique blog will capture the attention of a different reader if you take different approaches, but all will route them right to your website where you can sell them products and services, and capture their identity.

Capturing identities of people who visit your website can be done through inviting them to fill out forms and request information. It can also be done by inviting them to sign up for your newsletter which you can create and email to them through web services such as **Mailchimp.com**

Keeping and maintaining a website and blog can be an essential ingredient to a small business marketer's campaign.

Social Media Replaces the Traditional *Back Yard Fence*

Social media can best be defined as 'An online means of interaction among people where they create, share, exchange and connect with information about their lives, their ideas that sometimes includes commerce.' This definition is a hybrid composite from a variety of sources around the internet that attempts to define and quantify this new age of interaction on the internet.

It perhaps is easier to consider social media in the context of the replacement for the old 'backyard fence' where you leaned over occasionally and found out what was happening in the life of your neighbor.

The only difference is this new backyard fence spans the globe, and not only allows you to experience the sharing of ideas and events in the people's lives that you know, but also the lives of people you do not know. With each progressing day social media is creating a world with new dimensions of interacting with our fellow man.

As a small business marketer, the conventional former means of marketing and advertising through the printed newspaper and other forms of print are disappearing and giving way to the ease of use of the internet for information as well as in social media. Social media is now evolved into a vehicle to connect with people from all levels of society that were previously unreachable.

Celebrities, politicians, Chief Executive Officers of major corporations, sports figures, etc. are all within reach on social media. Whether or not they will interact with you is another story, however, millions upon millions of other people are within reach too. These people include much of your current customer base as well as future customer base.

It therefore becomes important to understand a little about Social Media in order to utilize it as a small business marketer.

There are numerous Social Media entities today across the internet. Some are more popular in certain corners of the world than others. Some are more of a niche group of interests or smaller communities. I have included a complete list of a majority of the common ones complete with links in the reference section at the back of this book. As time moves forward, there are always new ones coming into existence as the world of social media is ever changing.

The time spent on learning how to use social media and include it in ones marketing strategies is well worth it as the return on investment is greatest there is on the internet if one really engages in it. For the small business marketer, let's look at five of the larger and most popular forms of social media and how they can and should be used in marketing: **Facebook, Twitter, LinkedIn, YouTube** and **Pinterest**.

Once again there are far more social media entities, and I highly recommend that you explore the others on the list in the reference section in the back of this book. Let's take a look the big five that should be a part of any plan for small business marketers for the coming years ahead.

Facebook

Facebook.com is the largest social media and perhaps the best resource for demographic marketing ever created so far. It is more than just a place to interact with people, for the small business marketer it can be a goldmine of finding new clients if one really commits oneself to using it.

Let's examine the different aspects of Facebook:

The Personal Facebook Page

The personal page is where everyone starts on Facebook. The best practices are to make sure you have an informative profile filled out, a banner that defines you and use this to connect with friends. Examine what others in your business are doing and explore the best practices being used.

With the content you post, the best recommendation is to be positive. Express how you love your job, love the community and share friendly information. Avoid political debates, arguments or negative issues. Stay away from taking positions on controversial subject matters, and instead keep your personal page light and friendly and when possible informative.

Make sure if you choose to support a campaign of any kind that you select subject matters that are universally appealing to everyone and are considered 'unassailable' for someone to object to. Here are some examples of unassailable topics:

- Protecting children

- Caring for pets and helping animal shelters

- Caring for the elderly

- Gardening

- Cleaning up the environment such as litter pick up campaigns, etc.

- Home improvements

- Donating to or helping a charity

Additionally on your personal page, take time to explore Facebook in your community and click the 'like' button on local businesses and even in some cases people in the same profession as you that you might interact with, as in the case of Realtors, educators, etc.

Always take time to post as yourself on your personal page, rather than have someone else do it for you. Make the messages personal and real. Humor also works great, but make sure it is clean and light hearted in its content. You can share information from anywhere on the internet, including articles and pictures, but make sure you post a note along with it to make it personal.

Realize that whatever you share on Facebook or in any social media vehicle can usually be seen by anyone, so consider it a broadcast and make sure that broadcast reflects professionally on you and your business at all times. Additionally Facebook has rules established about promoting your business on your personal page. It is suggested you read the rules so you understand them, so that you do not violate them. If you are found to be in violation of the rules you can have your personal page cancelled.

Facebook Groups

There are many Facebook Groups out there. Find ones that interest you and join. Post messages or articles about your company, but make sure you read any group rules first. Some groups are more open to certain types of postings than others. Follow the rules or you will get booted and this can also become a negative on your business too.

People who frequent or run groups sometimes will toss out violators of the rules, and sometimes make an example of them by posting negative content about them. So be careful and ask permission from the group manager if you are uncertain if what you want to post is appropriate.

Facebook Groups can be created by anyone. If you do not find a group that suites your interests, then create your own. As a group administrator you can set the rules, promote and monitor the group. You can also add membership from your friend base, and they can opt out if they are not interested.

Groups allow you also to hold events and post information about your business if you are the administrator. You can also invite people to join as well by posting the link to your group on other similar like minded group pages, etc.

Facebook Business Pages

Facebook has established a vehicle for companies of all sizes to openly promote their businesses. It is called the *Facebook Business page*. Instead of building a membership as is done with a group, a business page is driven by 'Likes'.

As a small business marketer you should set yourself up a Facebook Business page and ask all your friends to 'Like' it. This is where it is important to build up a group of friends on your personal page. Once your business page has 30 'Likes' you can request a customized URL that reads as an example: **www.Facebook.com/'Yourcompanyname'.** This specialized title can be useful and important to use along with your website in advertising anywhere online or in print.

In setting up your business page, be sure to include a banner, a detailed profile of your business information, etc. If you have a retail or storefront of any kind, you might consider using a photo of this along with a photo of your company sign for starters. If you are your business, then a personal photo of you would be important to include as well.

Facebook business pages allow you also to create and post events. You can also use applications to schedule future postings of events and articles up to a year in advance, so it does not require that you be online every day. It becomes a great way to share constant information about your business.

Facebook business pages also offer a feature called '*Facebook insights*' where you can see statistics on the success of your page.

It will tell you right now how many people have seen your page that day, and in the future are expected to give you even more information including 'who' saw your page. This is a great feature to be able to monitor the progress and exposure of your business page.

Facebook mobile apps

Facebook can be accessed through most any mobile smart phone today. You can use apps to post to your personal page and also use apps to post to you business page. There are also apps and websites that allow you to post to multiple forms of social media which we discuss later in another chapter which allow you to schedule your social media out as far as one year in advance.

The important things to remember about posting from a mobile app to any form of social media is you be very careful about the auto-correct feature on most smart phones. There are settings that allow you to disable this if you choose on most phones. However, simply making sure you read through your post one last time before posting it is the best advice for a standard of practice. Large fingers on small key pads combined with the auto-correct feature can result in some unwanted and embarrassing messages being posted if you are not careful.

Facebook Advertising

Facebook also has one of the greatest and exciting forms of advertising ever created which can be utilized by the small business marketer. They allow businesses to post advertisements that target specific searching and profiles of people so that you can more precisely reach your clientele. If you are interested in posting an ad on Facebook, it is recommended that you click on the links for to post an ad and read the different terms available. A small business can use this method of advertising to reach new clients geographically and within precise demographics to create powerful advertising campaigns for very little money. Combined with the *Facebook Insights* feature, a small business marketer can easily monitor results.

Twitter

Twitter.com is a tool that can best be described as a *billboard* to the small business marketer. It has also been described as 'micro-blogging' with its limitations of 140 characters or less. It has become the resource of information that anyone can find connecting all forms of social media together. News media use this as a means of getting feedback from various people in society on topics of interest and current events.

Creating a twitter account is very simple and only requires an email to set it up. Once an account is created it becomes necessary to learn how to compose messages and what to '*Tweet*' as these messages are called.

What should you 'Tweet'?

For a small business one can tweet messages about all kinds of information on what is happening in and around your business. The important thing to understand is that whatever you tweet other people can see and find it, so make sure it is salient and important information that you would want people to know. Twitter is a vehicle to post not only messages, but also links for articles, videos, photos, etc. So if there is a current news story on your business, you can post the link, for an example. Here is a list of some types of items a small business marketer could consider for Tweets:

- Photos about the business and activities

- News articles

- Videos

- Coupons

- Events

- Product information

- Specials

- Any changes in the industry

- Updates of any kind

- Helpful tips

The #Hashtag

The 'Hashtag' (#) is the number symbol on your phone or computer keypad. It has become part of the Twitter language referred to as the *Hashtag*.

Placing the # symbol before a subject word or phrase such as **#Christmas, #Music** or **#Lovemydog** will enable people to search that *hashtag* word or phrase and find out what other people are tweeting about that subject.

As a twitter user you can create a *hashtag* about any subject and include it in your tweet. It may take some time for others to pick up on it and use it, but you can encourage your customers to tweet their satisfaction by using your hashtag for your business such as **#Joesgarage** or **#Lindasflowershop** as an example.

Hashtags allow you to trace certain subject matters and even research with twitter. Using this as a tool can give you a feel for what your customers are talking about or what is popular in general in the Twitter universe.

If you want to find out more about popular and common *Hashtags*, go to **Hashtagkey.com**.

Shortlinks

Links for certain articles and even videos can be quite long. Twitter limits you to 140 characters. This can sometimes prohibit you from talking about a subject and adding a link if the link is too long. To solve this, the '*short link*' was created. You can take any link on the internet and create a short link with it by using a link shortening tool. Simply search Google or Yahoo for 'URL Shortener' or 'Mini URL' and you will find one to use. It is a quick and easy tool to shorten a link and post it in a tweet.

Timing & Scheduling Your Tweets

To create a small business campaign for your company, you can prepare tweets and schedule them to tweet automatically in advance. The easy way to do this is to use websites and apps such as **Hootsuite.com** or **Tweetdeck.com**. These websites allow you to write your tweets out and schedule them in advance. You can tweet hourly, daily, weekly or monthly depending on your strategy. You can schedule tweets for up to a year in advance. There is no limit to the number of tweets your can schedule.

It should be noted that **Tweetdeck.com** limits you to tweeting your specific message only one time. So if you have a message you would like to repeat, then you either need to vary the wording slightly or use **Hootsuite.com.** Both *Hootsuite.com* and *Tweetdeck.com* allow you to use the application for free, but offer more product services if you pay for the upgrade.

There are other services that you should explore that allow you to schedule your tweets. Some are more sophisticated than others. Some charge for their services after a free trial, and others are free but offer more when you upgrade. Most all of these will allow you to send scheduled postings for **Twitter** and **Facebook** and some also for **Linkedin** and other social media. Be sure to read through the product descriptions, details and pricing and try them out before you commit. Find the one that is right for you.

Here is a list of some other scheduling websites for social media:

> **Twuffer.com**
>
> **Bufferapp.com**
>
> **SproutSocial.com**
>
> **StreamSend.com**
>
> **LaterBro.com**
>
> **Twaitter.com**
>
> **FutureTweets.com**

There are several more products out there and new ones being created all the time. Explore and use the one you are most comfortable with. Choose one that seems to work the best for your marketing campaign.

The most important aspect you are looking for is one that allows you to schedule your tweets weeks and months in advance and sends them reliably every time without error.

Twitter Mobile

You can use Twitter on your smart phone and post tweets through right from your phone. If you use this app, once again be sure to double check your tweets before you click send. Auto correct features on phones can change the entire meaning of your message and create an unprofessional appearance with your tweets. Also it is easy to make mistakes with large fingers on tiny key pads too.

Many of the Tweet scheduling software also offer mobile apps which allow you to work on future tweets right from your phone. So this can be a great time management tool to consider for downtime when you find yourself waiting for appointments, etc.

LinkedIn

LinkedIn.com is in fact one of the older more established social media websites, predating both *Twitter* and *Facebook*. This is a business networking service. The intended use if to create and connect with businesses through this professional networking social media service platform. **Linkedin** like *Facebook* offers groups and like *Twitter* allows you to post messages, articles, etc.

However you will find that the business groups and special subject groups are must more useful to you as a small business marketer. Here you will find groups that offer a wealth of professional experience and information in their discussions and postings. Consider Linkedin as a great resource for information, in addition to creating a professional profile for yourself and your company.

Linkedin also can serve as a professional network spanning many different companies for referrals to your business. Use it to post and share professional information about your company. Make sure your profile has not only your contact information, but also your achievements, awards, websites, blogs, etc. Use it as your professional calling card for presenting yourself before a professional community. Be willing to share leads with others as well.

One can also use **Hootsuite.com** to post messages to your Linkedin page. This can be a good way to share blog articles and the latest news about your business. Other professionals can also 'recommend' you as a professional in your field of expertise, and this can be an added advantage much like a 'Like' to a business page on Facebook.

YouTube

YouTube.com is sometimes overlooked with considering social media entities. However, it is in a whole new dimension of social media. **YouTube** uses videos as a way of creating interchange and sharing information. Millions of videos are uploaded and shared on **YouTube** daily.

This can be a great resource for you and your company to get out information about your products and services. Videos can be created and uploaded from a smart phone or laptop computer. There are all different levels of video editing software out there to help you get started with editing your own videos.

YouTube also has tools online that allow you to edit videos. If you want to invest in some professional video editing software and cameras, you can do that as well. In addition to that, you might consider hiring someone to create and produce them for you. However, this last method can be more expensive, but might be the best route for a truly professional presentation.

The best suggestion for finding the right method for you is to go to **YouTube** and watch videos on 'How to create videos' until you discover the method you are most interested in using for your marketing campaign. It is not as difficult as you think to create your own videos, and post them to YouTube. However for the more professional looking ones it does requires some time and a bit of study to do it right.

Pinterest

Pinterest.com is one of the newer social media networks that is catching on with large popularity so it is worth mentioning as it is fast becoming a very useful tool to the small business marketer.

Pinterest is a social media website that allows people to share photos and images with as much ease as Twitter. It allows you to organize items of interest in picture or image format, and share the things that you love and are inspired by in short descriptions of the images.

Small business marketers are using **Pinterest** to show photos of their products and include a link. One can also share images that are quotes in a picture form, and post those with a link as well. You can use **Pinterest** for commercial use, and they state on their website the following: "*If you want to use our Products for commercial purposes you must create a business account and agree to our Business Terms of Service.*"

So as with any form of social media, read the terms of use and follow the required practices for business to promote within their guidelines. Pinterest can be a great tool to share interesting images related to your company and install a link to more information billboards and redirect to other articles as well. It can also be a simple and easy way to create interest for your products and services.

Social Media in Summary

Social media is always evolving. One can say that the constant in social media is that there is no constant. *'Change'* is the only thing one can come to expect. Social media platforms grow and evolve, and some die off and are replaced by others that are new and more exciting.

The only way to stay ahead of the changes is to be involved actively in social media, and make a commitment to having it become an active part of your small business marketing plan. If you do not, then it will pass you by.

Always read the terms of service and use of the various social media platforms you are using. Follow the rules or they can terminate your account and you will risk losing all of your contacts. Try to use social media as a tool to meet new clients and stay in touch with former ones. It can also be a great tool to share positive information about what is happening in your business.

Social Media has grown to become such an integral part of the culture in this internet age that the small business marketer cannot ignore it. It is where people are spending their time, even at work. So if you want to reach them you need to be where the customer can be found. Social media is where the people are spending their time, and this is where you should as well in order to reach out to them.

There are specialized social media groups that focus on artists, website developers, music lovers, book readers, photography, etc. More are developing as this book is written and some that are mentioned here may not be around in 5 years, who knows? The world of social media as well as companies online that support them are always changing, merging and dissolving. So the only way to really stay on top of the changes is to use it, and find the ones that work best for you and your business. With social media, if you do not enjoy it, you will find it difficult to use it as part of your routine. So find ones that you love and run with it.

Online Advertising

To begin a campaign as a small business marketer, there are a few basic tips on can start with immediately. Most involve promoting your website, so taking some of these steps make more sense after a website is already established:

Claim your spot on Google Places - Get setup with Google Places. 'Google Places' is a feature connected with the mapping application on Google that lets local businesses post contact information about your business. It is very simple, just go to 'Google Places' and fill out all your local online business information. Include photos, coupons, product offerings, or videos. In description fields, insert some of your keywords (within moderation).

Create "About Us" and "Contact Us" pages on your website to target local customers - Add your local business hours, directions, and contact info. This content serves to reinforce your location with search engines.

Get your business rated - Good reviews can bring huge boosts to your business. Encourage reviews by asking for feedback through your Facebook and Twitter accounts.

Focus on social media- Social media has been proven to be increasingly important factor when it comes to ranking for local search, so be sure to regularly update your Facebook and Google+ accounts.

Get your business listed in directories- Get your business listed in a number of online local directories, providing reputable links that can improve your local online search ranking.

Get citations in directories such as:

Yelp: www.yelp.com

SuperPages: www.superpages.com

CitySearch: www.citysearch.com

TrueLocal: www.truelocal.com

Express Update: www.expressupdateusa.com

Citysquares.com: www.citysquares.com

MojoPages.com: www.mojopages.com

InfoUSA: www.infousa.com

DMOZ:www.dmoz.org

BOTW: www.botw.org

Business.com: www.business.com

Also get your business listed in local directories like your Better Business Bureau and local Chamber of Commerce.

'Pay per Click' (PPC) Advertising

Once the above is completed, you may also want to explore 'Pay per click' advertising, also referred to as 'PPC' advertising. PPC advertising is essentially buying ads online which will drive business to your website or blog. It is a model of advertising where you pay every time a customer clicks through on the ad wherever it is posted.

This kind of advertising can be keyword and geographically connected so when an internet browser is searching a topic related to your ad, your ad then shows up on the webpage they are on encouraging them to click to find out more. The click on the ad of course takes them to your website.

With search engines, advertisers typically bid on keyword phrases relevant to their target market they are seeking to attract. Content sites commonly charge a fixed price per click rather than use a bidding system.

These advertisements are purchased in blocks based on this fee. PPC "display" advertisements, also commonly known as "banner" ads, are shown on web sites or search engine results with related content that have agreed to show ads. The idea being that when a prospective buyer types in your keyword your ad shows up to persuade them to click through to your website.

A common resource is to go through Google using their AdWords feature to bid on keywords in your local market, and place your advertisement. You purchase blocks of monetary units which are used up as people click on your display advertisement.

The idea is that is drives business into your website. This of course can be seen with more immediate results with purchases of your products on your website, increased visitors to your website and with all hopes results in people contacting your company. It serves as a great way to increase exposure of your website, as well as boost your online sales.

Another great resource for local businesses is to utilize Facebook advertising. Very much like the PPC model of search engines, Facebook advertising can target a geographic location and give you broader exposure for your products and services.

People commonly use Facebook as a means of social recreation, and quite often they mention things going on in their life on their personal page. These postings often include keywords that can result in your ad popping up on their page to inspire them to click through. Also, if they search on Facebook for a subject these keywords will create the same result.

For example, let's say your business is a veterinarian clinic. You pay for a local PPC ad on Facebook. When people in your local area post messages using your selected keywords for 'Dogs', 'Cats', 'Puppies', etc. your ad will pop up as a local veterinarian clinic. This creates a personalized exposure for your company, and can offer you access to a very precise target audience.

Monetizing your website or blog

Not only can you purchase advertising space online to draw business to your website, you can also post advertisements on your websites and blogs that help to generate money for your efforts. This is called 'Monetizing' a website or blog.

There are basically two general categories of ads one can run on a website or blog. There are the PPC ads, and the other type which are product specific ads.

PPC ads are offered by websites like *Google Adwords* where you sign up and agree to post one of their ads on your website. This type of advertising can have its benefits and negatives.

The benefits are that they will often pull up ads related to your content and if these ads align with what you are promoting, it is okay.

The negative is that these ads can also pull up your competition and display them on your page. They can also pull up PPC ads that you would not want to see on your website that might be offensive to your customers such as ads for 'checking criminal backgrounds' showing someone's mug shot, etc.

With product specific ads you can go to websites such as Amazon and choose the products you want to advertise on your website or blog.

So if your blog is about nature trials to boost your business which is selling hiking and outdoor equipment, then you could choose an ad from Amazon to display of books about hiking for example.

If you have a flower shop and you could go to Amazon and choose to post a product specific ad featuring books on poetry or a display ad for featuring jewelry, etc.

Here are some websites you can visit to for resources for online advertising:

www.Clickbank.com

www.Google.com/adwords

www.Affiliate.Program.Amazon.com

Email & Text Messaging

Since the world has progressively begun to communicate faster and faster through means of email and text messaging, this is another area where the small business marketer can overlook the value of tying this in with the overall marketing strategy.

E-mail Marketing

With every email one should create a signature that promotes your business. If you use programs like Outlook, they allow you to add not only phone number and fax numbers, but also active links. One should as a minimum place an active link to the company website in the signature line of your email.

Here is a list of suggested information to include in your email signature:

- *Your name*

- *Your company website*

- *You phone number*

- *Your company address*

- *Your fax number*

- *Your Twitter handle (with an active link)*

- *Your Facebook page (with an active link)*

- *A positive phrase or message about your business*

- *Motivational or memorable quotes*

- *Other social media*

One does not necessarily need to include all of the above, as every business approach is different. However, not taking the opportunity to include some basic contact information in your standard email reply signature or your origination email signature is losing an opportunity to share you info with them. Sometimes people forward interesting email and it may be the only way you can connect with the forwarding party is by having them call you back after reading it.

Email signatures can be set up with most any smart phone or tablet PC as well. When working from a desktop computer, Outlook lets you set up several different email signatures which you can save and use for whatever purpose you set up.

You can also set up an email signature with a standard information response that you reply with for circumstances where people write in for information about a topic. Create an answer for frequently asked questions to specific topics in your batch of signatures and it is just a click away from getting them the answers they need.

Additionally using programs like outlook, one can set up auto-reply emails with information for after hour responses that let the sender know their email was received and if the matter is urgent, they can call you on the phone, etc.

These automated messages can be set up and changed daily or hourly as you need to. You can also set up an automated email for a specific email address to send information they request on an automatic response.

If you consider your email signature and auto-reply feature as a marketing tool, one can quickly see the potential of using these features.

Text Message & Email on Smartphones

Most anyone who has a smart phone has used text messages to relay a communication to someone at some point. Some people use it more than others. It really is a matter of preference. There are ways to include a tag line or signature similar to email on a smart phone. One way to include a 'one line message' standard along with every text is by cutting and pasting this information from a note pad when you want to add you contact information on a text.

Another way on the iPhone is if you go to your settings and look under '*General*' settings, then go to '*keyboard*' then to '*short cuts*' you can set up a phrase in your shortcuts that will pop up automatically if you set up a shortcut of 2 or 3 letters or characters.

This way you can have a phrase for use in texting or email such as '*Your hometown resource for all your plumbing needs*' or '*Your friend in the diamond business*' without having to type it in every time. You just type in your preset shortcut combination that you set up and it will insert your phrase immediately. This can make sending a rapid text or email message with your tag line easy.

Additionally on the iPhone, for example, they typically include a standard line that reads '*Sent from my iPhone*' as signatures for email. You can change this in your *settings* under '*Mail*' then '*Signature*'. You can also create a different signature for every separate email account you have, if you have multiple accounts.

Droid phones and Samsung phones have similar features to allow you to insert email signatures and shortcuts.

Change the signature to include you website, phone number, twitter handle, etc. Use it for whatever promotional marketing information you want to share. It takes just a few moments to set up and you can change it as often as you like. This can be a simple way to send information quickly, and tie in your daily messages with the rest of your ongoing marketing campaign.

The Power of Reaching Out

"Speech is power: speech is to persuade, to convert, to compel."

-Ralph Waldo Emerson

Whether one holds an event and brings in speakers, or does public speaking oneself, there is an advantage to sharing one's wisdom with others. Self-publishing a book or eBook is also a form of public speaking and the sharing of knowledge. It all hinges on good public relations and then it becomes the power to drive a business to new heights of recognition and positioning as the authority in the marketplace.

In this section we will explore the power of reaching out within the community your business works in and *persuade, to convert* and *to compel* others to do business with your company as a marketing tool.

Hosting an Event

If you have a small business location that you are marketing, it can pay off to host a private or open public event at your location. Special events can draw traffic to the location that can result in future sales and a raised public awareness of your business.

There are two basic categories of events.

1) New business opening events

2) Established business events

Within each of these two categories there can be both *private* and *public* events which can open the door to new customers and clientele.

A private event involves inviting a specialized group of people generally through personal invitation. An open public event generally involves much more fanfare and promotion to draw anyone who will come.

Setting up a Successful Private Event

Setting up a private event requires coming up with something to draw interest. It also requires having a mailing list to send invitations to. These invitations can be sent to a list of personal friends, or a select group of people in a particular category. One can acquire a mailing list as discussed in the earlier chapter on Direct Mail. Select a group of people that are likely to respond to your personal invitation.

Drawing Interest

Drawing interest to the event requires what is coined in public relations circles as a 'gimmick'. 'Gimmicks' are usually intriguing things that will capture someone's interest and compel them to arrive. Here are some ideas of gimmicks for a private 'invitation only' event that can draw people:

- A celebrity or some other popular public figure

- A wine tasting

- A private chef cooking some unique food

- Good food or cuisine

- A magician

- Musicians & music

- A unique form of entertainment

- A special lecture on a topic of interest

- A popular cause

- A radio personality

- A contest or reward

- An awards ceremony (where the invitees are likely recipients)

- A special private unveiling of something new and never before seen

- A mystery to invite imagination

The above is just a list of ideas that have proven to work. There is no limit to the creativity once you start brainstorming on it. The essential characteristic of a good private event is that the feature or 'Gimmick' is *too irresistible to pass up.*

It is always important to have something that keeps people there as well. Food is always a good draw and can keep people around. The same goes for a wine tasting or popular personality.

One can look at the list above and incorporate more than one in the same event to make it even more compelling to attend.

One should of course have staff of your business present and displays or information available about your company for all guests. Present the information in a tactful manner as part of a gift when they arrive, information brochure, etc.

It is important that such events start on time, and end on the time as well. One should also check invitations at the door to make sure at least the illusion of exclusivity is presented even if you do not want to be strong on the enforcement of it.

An example of a private event I once held in my Decorative Glass Company in Atlanta was the following:

We invited a well known and high priced interior decorator to come in and do a presentation. We sent out RSVP invitations to a select group of clients that we had sold to before, and asked them to bring a neighbor with them. We set up a slide projector and screen, and invited our designer to do a talk on interior decorating.

As an introduction to the speaker, we presented a short ten minute slide show on stained and decorative glass applications for the home, showing photos and providing them free information. We also included some small amounts of food and snacks from a local catering company, along with some coffee and tea. All attendees left with a special folder which included business cards, flyers, coupons, etc. from our company and our guest speaker. We also had a violinist playing in the reception before the event started. We started on time, and ended on time.

The events were held around 7pm each time. We held this and similar events over a period of six months with different speakers. Each event we had approximately 20 to 25 attendees. This size of group made it possible to answer questions, and interact with them socially on a more personal level. The end result was that both our speaker and our company got business from the event, and it became a regular part of our successful actions.

This event came about from a brainstorming of our sales staff and surveying our customers. They were always well attended and the word of mouth spread the more we did them. We invited people from specific neighborhoods as well as our from our own customer files to generate more repeat business as well.

There can be many variations on such an event, and it does not have to become too costly. There is always some cost and a preparation involved, but the outcome can be well worth it.

Here is an example of an event held by the Public Relations Director at Atlanta Homes & Lifestyles Magazine in the 1990's:

A contest was held in the magazine for interior designers to submit photos of their work for a contest. The magazine staff would review the entries and give out awards in different categories, as well as one large overall award for 'Designer of the year'.

They then set up the event at the small business of one of their advertisers and held an awards ceremony. When interviewing the PR director afterwards he said "If you ever want to have 100% attendance, hold an awards ceremony and invite a large group of potential winners'. So this was the format for their event.

They of course had food, wine, music and a lot of fanfare. They gave out awards in numerous categories from 'Best

Contemporary Design', 'Most Original Design', 'New Trend Setting Design', 'Best Traditional Design', etc. Of course there was also the overall prize of 'Designer of the Year' as well. It was a great event and a packed house.

The event was held in the showroom of a kitchen design company, and they of course benefited from the exposure to all of the city's best interior designers that evening in their newly opened showroom. As a result, they continued to advertise with Atlanta Homes & Lifestyles Magazine, and the magazine also signed up new clients that night too because they invited prospective advertisers to attend the exclusive ceremony and meet the cities top designers.

Holding a Successful Open Public Event

Public events are ones where you are trying to draw people from a larger base, and are not selective about where they come from; you are just trying to generate broad exposure for your business. These can be great events for launching a new business or just giving a boost to an already established business.

Once again having a 'gimmick' that will appeal or attract the broad masses is essential. One needs to set up the event so that it will attract people from visual drive-by, radio & television, print media and other forms of display advertising. One cannot take an 'ordinary' approach and expect people to pay notice. The small business marketer needs to think like a three ring circus and try to attract customer attention units on many levels.

Here are a few creative and radical ideas that have proven to be attention getting. Use as many as you can, and also explore and look for other creative methods when you find them:

- Radio broadcast - Quite often radio stations in the area

can be contracted to come and do a live broadcast from your store. These can vary in price, depending on the size and popularity of the radio station. This usually involves a radio personality or personalities broadcasting their entire show or a portion of it live from your business. They of course invite people to come visit them and see your business, take part in the live show, etc. This is quite a fun way to draw people. It is suggested that you do a survey of any existing customers you might have and find out what radio stations they listen to. Radio stations tend to appeal to different demographics, and their advertising department should be able to provide you with information on this.

- Radio 'Prize Patrol' - This is a step down from an actual broadcast. Many radio stations have a van with their logo on it that travels around and sets up at businesses in the area. They call into the station during broadcasts and let people know where they are located and ask them to come on down to win cool prizes. The advantage of a prize patrol is that they often are a lot less costly to procure, and sometimes they can stay longer.

- Spotlight - If you are hosting an event in the evening, then a spot light can be an incredible way to attract attention. There are companies that rent huge spotlights that usually are on a trailer or vehicle and they bring this to the store, and shoot the beam of light from your parking lot into the sky. This works best on a clear night or a semi-clear night when there is a low cloud cover in the sky. This kind of gimmick brings the curious to investigate what is going on, so it is important to tie this in with other things that will draw them into the parking lot or compel them to stop at the store when they arrive.

- Specialty Signage - Everyone loves a 'Sale'. The word 'Sale' may sound overdone, but in fact it is so ingrained in the psyche of the average shopper that it is a great draw. It works best to place these signs where they can appear temporary and also obvious. You might be surprised that a hand drawn 'Sale' sign will quite often attract more curious buyers in some smaller businesses than a pre-made one. It can give the impression of it being individual and unique in the right circumstance. Large fabric banners tied across the front of the store or flapping in the wind are also great ways to draw people. Just make sure that were ever you place them, that they are visible from both close and far away. Different sizes of signs are also important to accomplish this, and pointing in different directions.

- Skywriting - There are still some companies that do sky writing with small airplanes. This can be an interesting draw, however due to the limitations of the skywriter and fuel it usually limits you to a one to three word message. So if your business has a short recognizable name, you might pay someone to sky write 'Sale at ___' in the sky. This kind of gimmick of course is limited to a clear sky day, so can be difficult to schedule.

- Airplane banner towing - This is often an easier and less expensive option than skywriting. A small airplane will tow a banner behind it with your message in circles in the sky around your store. This can be another great curiosity draw from long distances on a clear day. Choose a bright colored banner and a bold readable message to advertise your event and let it fly.

- Inflatable displays - There are companies that set up large inflatable animals of all kinds to serve as big bold and crazy temporary signs for events such as this. There is also the large inflatable houses that independent vendors can set up to charge admission for kids to jump around inside.

- Set up a small carnival - If you have the advantage of a large parking lot or field adjacent to your business, consider setting up small one to two day carnival. There are companies that travel around and do this for auto dealerships and other businesses, and it can become an instant event that requires little preparation on your part. The often come complete with rides, displays and other attractions.

- Moving signage - There are several simple rentable signage displays that are often available through a local rental center. A particularly good one to attract drive-by attention is the portable fan that blows upwardly through wind sock shaped like a cartoon man. It flops back and forth in the intermittent wind of the fan, and has great movement to attract attention to what is going on. It helps to flank such an item with clear signage about your event to that when people look, they get the message and are compelled to stop.

- Balloons - There are many types of balloons one can use to attract attention. One can simply rent a small helium tank and blow up multi-colored balloon and tie them all over. There is also the Mylar style balloon which is silver in color that reflects sunlight and moves in the wind. Then there are the large balloons one can inflate and tether and have it floating 300+ feet in the sky. Additionally one can contact local hot air balloonists and have one or more hot air balloons inflated in your parking area in front of your business. Sometimes they can be arranged to give tether rides as an additional draw. Balloons can be magic and have broad appeal.

- Celebrity Booking - Another great public drawing gimmick is to have a celebrity on hand to sign autographs. Contact a local sports or celebrity booking company like *www.UniversalAttractions.com* or *www.CommndTalent.com* to choose the one that will be the right personality draw for your business. They can range from actors, media personalities to local professional sports players. There are many such companies, and prices for this vary depending on the popularity of the personality you hire. Two important things to consider in taking this approach: One, make sure you survey your customer demographics to choose the right personality for that demographic. Two, be certain to verify that the personality you hire has a reputation of showing up on time and not cancelling. Nothing can torpedo a public relations event more destructively than to have a celebrity you contract cancel at the last minute and ruin your event.

- Freebies - Giving away free items can be a great draw, especially if it is a highly desirable or popular item. 'Free Beer and Hot Wings' or 'Enter to win a Free Tractor' etc can be great gimmicks. I would caution any business owner on giving away free alcohol products; however, as there can be considerable liability with this should someone leave your event and have an alcohol related accident on their way home. It can also require special permits from your local municipality to do this. However there are a lot of other great food items that can be a draw such as: *chili, fried chicken, boiled peanuts, bagels, sandwiches, steak, hamburgers, hotdogs, hot apple cider, coffee, hot chocolate, lemonade, ice cream, etc.* that can just as attractive in the right circumstance and make for a fun event. Sometimes hiring a few food vendors to set up portable booths in front of your store can also be a great draw. Prizes and contests also work well as a 'freebie' draw, and can be promoted to hold drawings throughout the day to get people to stay longer and enter to win. A popular giveaway is often an iPad or computer item, for example. Holding a sign-up entry contest can also be a great way to collect identities for future marketing, which will be discussed later in this book.

- Music - Music can be another great draw. One can hire a DJ or hire a series of bands and promote them as part of the event. One can also have single musicians to play background music while people tour the store, such as a pianist, cellist, violinist or guitar player. It all depends on the theme and taste of your event, but music can be a great way to keep people around and draw them to the event as well. What is important to consider when choosing to use this option is that one choose a source a musical entertainment that will be popular to the demographics you are servicing and reaching out to in your business.

- Invitations - Invitations can be sent out as a direct mail piece to a surrounding demographic area or to a select group. It is important to time this promotion to arrive at least 1-2 days before the event in their mail box. If doing multiple mailings (which is preferred for greater success) then arrange for the first piece arrive one week before the event, and the others within the following days to keep the reminder present in their minds. Be sure to include all the details of your event that can be expected: food, music, and personalities, balloon rides, etc. whatever is appropriate.

This is a list of ideas that can be used, and it is always good advice to examine other events held by businesses in your area that drew a lot of people to mimic what they are doing. If one does not have the patience to organize such an event, there often are companies that you can hire to make all the arrangements and do all of the planning for you so you can just focus on being ready and selling your products.

Events can take a lot of preparation, but in the long run can be well worth it for the continuous exposure they can create for a business. It is recommended to have an event of some kind planned for your business as a part of your marketing plan at least every quarter on your calendar, if not more frequently. The more you do, the more you will see the results and magic. You will also learn what works and what does not work for your business through practical experience in doing them, and your future events will become better and better.

Final Suggestions

Whenever you hold an event, it is suggested you keep a written record of some kind. The best way to do this is to keep a log book. A log book become useful in the long term for the small business marketer, as one can refer back to it and repeat what work. One can also use it as a way to recall all the important details of what went into the planning and preparation.

Therefore in keeping a log, it is always better to record as much detail about the preparation, planning and what the outcome was as possible. It is better to keep this log record as you go along in preparing for the event, and to make notes immediately following the conclusion of the event while details are fresh in your mind. Make notes of not only what you did to prepare for it, but what attendance you received, how the public responded, how long it went, what the weather conditions were, etc.

All of these details can be important to have recorded when doing multiple events and re-visiting them several months or even a year or two down the road. It becomes easy to repeat exactly what worked in the past when one has a record of what happened. Additionally if you are hosting the event at your showroom, have attendees sign a guest book when they arrive and ask them to provide their name, address, phone and email. This can be a valuable tool for prospecting to these former attendees later on.

Speaking Engagements

Public speaking is not something that appeals to everyone. However, if you can overcome your nerves and take on the challenge it can be a very creative way to raise the awareness of your business in the community. The challenge in public speaking is finding an audience to speak to. There are several ways to go about this.

Speaking Before Established Community Groups

To begin, as discussed before there are many service clubs within a community that one can join. These types of clubs often are looking for people to speak at luncheons and therefore offer opportunities for public speaking. Sometimes it is just to the group members themselves at certain times of the year, and other times they have opportunities for members to represent the group on topics of interest along with other groups. Getting involved with the leadership of a business or trade organizations sometimes offers speaking opportunities as well.

What one is trying to do in public speaking is to find a topic of interest to speak about, and then sell a group of people on the idea to let you come speak about it. It can be related to your business and its products, but it can also be on an indirect or non-related topic such as business market conditions in an area or industry trends.

For example, if one has a sporting goods store, one could speak on a related topic of being an active proponent of the new '*heads up football program*' sponsored by the National football League which encourages the teaching of kids playing football to keep their heads up to avoid neck injury later on by developing unsafe playing practices.

One could also talk about changes in the coaching strategies you have seen over the years, or new franchise sports teams coming to the area. One could also speak on a non-related topic such as the street improvements for your business community.

Each speaking opportunity offers you a chance to get your name out there as the business spokesperson, as well as raising awareness of your business in the community.

Sometimes the press will cover such events and quote you, and reference what business you are from. As long as you avoid controversial topics that could create a negative response from some readers of the newspaper or watchers of the television broadcast, this can be good exposure for your company.

Guest Speaking on a local Radio Show

Another way to reach people as a speaker representing your business is to contact a local radio station and request to come on as a guest. There are two basic approaches to take when trying to become a guest on such a radio show.

1) **The professional Expert:** Taking the position as a professional expert on a subject related to your business. For example, if the local radio station has a Saturday morning program on gardening and your business is related to gardening or lawn care in some way, this is an easy sell to get yourself on as a guest speaker. There quite often are home improvement shows, pet shows and other community interest shows that with a little imagination you can position your professional background and approach the station managers about having you on as a guest.

2) **The Community Project:** There are many charitable organizations and projects one can get involved in within the community. Take an active role in such a group and volunteer also to be their guest spokesperson on a radio show. Many times you will find that either no one considered doing that or that other members are too shy to take on such a task. Being a volunteer at the Humane Society for example could open the door for you to speak on the local radio show weekly, and also mention your business and why your business has decided to back this effort, etc. It is good public relations and helps to throw your company name out there, your name as a spokesperson raising awareness of who you are in the community, and helping to build a positive image for your company as well.

Smaller radio stations are sometimes looking for fresh ideas and guest speakers. Taking a chance and talking to a station manager on the idea could be a good way to create some positive exposure for your business. If they like you, they might also invite you back.

Create Your Own Events

Another way to expand on public speaking is to create your own event as discussed in a previous chapter on events. This can be a great way to get started and practice before smaller groups.

Try also speaking at your church or other organizations you might be involved in. Sometimes a business product or service can appeal to a niche group such as the elderly. In a case like that, try contacting a local retirement activity center and arrange to do a presentation.

Ask Your Customers

Another resource for finding groups and organizations to be a guest speaker for is to ask your customers. Survey them to find out what groups they are a part of, and see if there is interest in any of the groups they are part of to have speakers.

You might be surprised at how easy this is to do.

By taking the time to survey your satisfied customer base, you might gain access to speaking a church groups, civic groups, service clubs, sporting clubs, etc.

Sometimes with these groups you would never have been successful in approaching directly, but because a member referred you, you receive an invitation.

The Benefits of Taking Time for Public Speaking in the Community

Taking time for public speaking within your community helps to raise the awareness of your company and your spokesperson. It also is beneficial if you have multiple spokespersons representing the company spanning different genres and genders. By raising public awareness and name recognition for your company, you can build upon a positive company image. This can help spread positive word of mouth, especially if people really connect with you as a speaker and you inspire them.

Any public speaking you do should have a degree of an entertainment factor and fund factor. Dull, dry and boring presentations although they may be informative are not often memorial. What you want to accomplish in a speaking engagement is that they remember you and your company. If they learn something new or you solve their problem for them is important, but what is more important is that they remember your name and company and do so in a positive manner.

One way to learn how to be a good public speaker is to study other public speakers. Go to speaking engagements and observe the styles of other speakers, and also take note of how the audience responds to them. Another resource for studying public speakers is to watch video recordings of speakers on YouTube. Watch videos on a variety of topics and once again listen to how they do their presentation, observe the audience and also take note of your own reaction to them. Do they keep you interested? Would you want to see them speak again? All of these points are important factors. Emulate the better speakers as best you can and you will be on the right track to developing a style of your own that people want to listen to.

You will find that when you have done a few presentations as a speaker around the community and it is memorable, the more you do the more people will seek you out to speak for other groups. Word of mouth will spread, and new opportunities will open up for you and your marketing team.

Self-Publishing

There is no greater expert position one can assume that to be the person who '*wrote the book on the subject*'. If your industry or product line has never released a book, you should seriously consider self-publishing your own books.

Publishing a book is not such a difficult or challenging a task as it was a decade ago. There are many companies that will help you publish your books for free and sell them as 'print on demand'. You always have the option to pay them for their services, but they also provide step by step instructions on how to do it yourself.

This can be a huge cost saver if you have the time. Print on demand is essentially just as it sounds. A customer orders a book, and it is actually printed as a single book and delivered to them. No longer are you required to print 50,000 copies to get your book published. You can publish just one book, and sell it on Amazon, Barnes and Noble or other publishing sites and have the book shipped immediately to the buyer within a few days.

It does take some time to read through the required steps and apply them. It will require that you have a computer to write, prepare and even design the cover for the book.

The terms and services will vary depending on what company you use. Here is a list of popular self-publishing websites to look into and find the one that works best for your needs:

www.createspace.com

www.lulu.com

www.outskirtpress.com

www.iuniverse.com

www.authorhouse.com

www.blurb.com

www.shopmybook.com

The option available to you as a self-publisher is to publish an eBook. EBooks are becoming more and more popular and the portability and immediate delivery places information at people's finger tips within minutes. EBooks can be marketed through your website and also sold broadly to the public on Amazon, Barnes and Noble and though Apple.

Here is a breakdown of self-publishing websites for eBooks:

>**Smashwords:** *www.Smashwords.com*

>**Lulu:** *www.lulu.com*

>**Amazon***: www.kdp.amazon.com*

>**Barnes & Noble:** *www.nookpress.com*

Having a published book or eBook in your marketing plan of attack adds a lot of credibility to you as a public speaker as well as a spokesperson for your business. It can be published from a single author or a company. The published book offers credibility and a sense of authority on the subject, especially when your competition does not have a published book.

Being a published author also opens doors to getting into the public eye with book signings, radio shows as a guest and even as a public speaker. It can be an incredible boost to a marketing campaign for a small business, and today is does not have to cost you anything but some time to write and create it. You only pay the publisher a fee when the book sells. You also get paid a royalty on every sale. So this can also become a way to fund a marketing campaign as well.

A published book can give you the expert position. Publishing more than one book can add even more credibility. It can be an incredibly valuable tool to give your business the edge and at the same time build a readership and reach more people. 'How to' books can also be tied in with a YouTube promotional channel as well as be offered as a free give to customers. However you want to use it, having a published book can have a number of incredible uses in a marketing campaign. Just let your imagination run with it!

Good Public Relations Practices

'Public relations' is how people see and regard you and your company ultimately in the end. Public relations could best be defined as: *"The professional maintenance of a favorable public image by an organization or a famous person."*

As a small business marketer, one must become cognizant of all aspects of public relations as it will impact your present and future business. Customer service is at the base of all public relations problems for most small companies. Not servicing the customer or not resolving an upset with a disgruntled customer in the past perhaps did not impact one's business as much as it does today. The old adage that one upset customer will tell five other people used to be all one had to worry about. Now in the age of the internet, one upset customer will tell thousands and their complaint will be available to be seen by millions.

It really is unfair for many businesses when they get someone who writes vicious online review of their company. This one person is one voice, yet sometimes it is the only voice who takes time to write a review on a website.

In fact, one can argue that most of the online negative reviews are written by someone who is motivated to retaliate against the business in some way, and in truth negates to reflect upon all the other happy customers who are out there using that company's products and services.

Good public relations practices become a major necessity in the age of the internet. One must develop a proactive approach to it, as opposed to a reactive approach.

Solicit happy customers for good reviews

To combat bad reviews online, one should take a proactive approach and ask happy customers to write positive reviews about your company. Why wait for some lone nut to decide to become malicious and attack your company on the internet. Many times they are complete idiots who enjoy doing nothing better than causing harm to a company's reputation on the internet.

There are several ways one can combat this.

- Educate your employees to request that happy customers write a positive online review about your business on website such as 'Yelp'. Give them a coupon for a free service or discount if they do.

- Call up old familiar customers and friends and ask them to write a positive online review as well.

- Set up a computer in the store or showroom and have people write a short post while they are in the store on your website or on Yelp while they are there in the store. Give them a discount or some other gift if they take to time to share their experience with others before they leave.

The best solution for a negative online review is to bury it with tons of positive ones. This makes that negative person stand out as a lone nut, and they lose credibility.

Another important practice to get into is to ask your satisfied customers to write a short note or letter while they are in the store or when the product is delivered which shares their satisfaction. This is a common practice with restaurants with survey cards. Include a small box on the paper that they can check if the story is okay for you to use in marketing to share with others.

This gives you as the small business marketer an opportunity to collect a large file over time of happy customer letters to use in all forms of marketing. Nothing speaks to new prospective customers better than a testimonial from a former customer. These success stories and testimonials can and should be added to your website, blogs and all forms of print publications.

This practice should become a regular tool one uses to keep new and continuous good news reports about your company online.

Post Positive Videos Online

Using YouTube to post positive videos about your business

should also be a standard practice. Create videos of customer testimonials as well as information about your products and services. Post new videos regularly to build up a following on your channel.

Educate Company Owners and Employees

Positive 'public relations' practices require that everyone in the company understand the importance of good customer service and its negative consequences. Not only are unsatisfied customers going to the internet with reviews, the world has gone more and more video with the age of YouTube. Pranksters and idiots love to video people without telling them, baiting them into some situation, and then later post the video on YouTube.

YouTube pays channel owners money for videos that get more than 10,000 views. Sensationalized videos are all over the site. Don't let your business become a target this kind of thing. Educate your owners and employees to conduct themselves in an appropriate manner as if they are being secretly recorded whenever there is the slightest doubt.

If you have an upset customer, use common sense in dealing with it. Sometimes you run into the criminal element that is really trying to steal and get a free service at your company's expense. It is better in most cases to settle the matter amicably rather than confrontationally.

If necessary give them their money back, take the losses and send them on their way. Use your judgment on this, but remember that public relations errors can cost you a lot in defense and lost customers down the road if the person becomes vicious with your company online.

It is never easy navigating through a situation with an upset customer. Not everyone is cut out for it. It is better for public relations and marketing quite often to have a person assigned as a specialist in the company to deal with such matters. Assign someone to the task that has tremendous patience and is not easily riled.

Promote Positive Image Stories

As part of your marketing plan you should endeavor to get good news stories created with your company being mentioned as discussed in an earlier chapter. Once you have these stories, take some copies of the news paper and clip the article and headline of the newspaper showing the date and newspaper name and paste them up on a sheet.

Make copies of the articles and promote these good news stories to customers, post them on bulletin boards and share them online. Make sure the good image created in the article is shared on all of your communication lines. Do this every time you have a news article published on your company. Share this information with your own employees as well so they can tell their families. This is all part of the good public relations.

In addition to sharing the information, create a press book with original copies of the articles pasted up in them. Make this book available to sales people, marketing personnel and even in the reception of your showroom or place of business.

Follow the Golden Rule

Finally, in all actions in dealing with anyone, follow the golden rule: *Try to treat others as you would like to be treated. Do unto others as you would have them do unto you.* Whatever version or whatever wording, live this rule and you will have a good understanding of what positive public relations practices consist of.

The Power of Broadcasting

"To those who say people wouldn't look; they wouldn't be interested; they're too complacent, indifferent and insulated, I can only reply: There is, in one reporter's opinion, considerable evidence against that contention. But even if they are right, what have they got to lose?

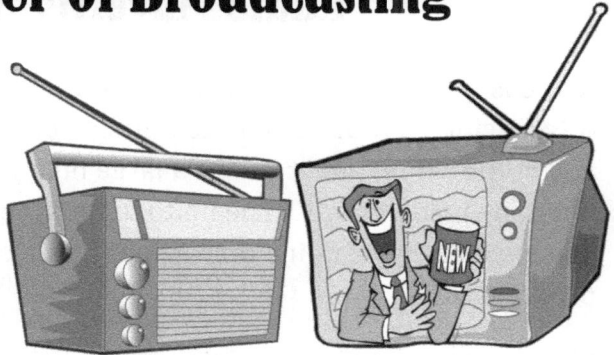

Because if they are right, and this instrument is good for nothing but to entertain, amuse and insulate, then the tube is flickering now and we will soon see that the whole struggle is lost.

This instrument can teach, it can illuminate; yes, and it can even inspire. But it can do so only to the extent that humans are determined to use it to those ends. Otherwise it is merely wires and lights in a box. Good night and good luck."

-Edward R Murrow, on the dawn of the age of television broadcasting

Radio, Television and YouTube comprise today's largest source of broadcast media. Broadcast media can be advantageous and also expansive for the small business marketer.

There are definite 'dos' and 'don'ts' to utilizing these resources in a marketing campaign. The following section of chapters will explore some successful actions one can take in these mediums.

Radio Advertising

Radio is the oldest form of broadcast media in the world. Advertising on radio can be advantageous for some businesses and at the same time it can be a large hole you throw money into if it done incorrectly. To begin to understand radio advertising, one must really examine the various nuances of radio programming.

First, there is a different audience at different hours of the day. One could safely break down a weekly radio time schedule to three largely different time groupings: Daytime, Nighttime and weekends. These can then be broken down into smaller increments of time such as daytime being broken down into morning drive (6am - 9am), late morning (9am -noon) noontime (noon - 3pm) and afternoon (3pm - 6pm). Evening can be broken down into early evening (5-9pm), late night (9pm - midnight) and graveyard (midnight to 6am). Weekends are broken down into days and nights, Saturday and Sunday. Programming for each radio station will vary depending on the time of day and time slot.

There are many different types of programming appealing to many different listening audiences. Some examples of the common ones are: talk radio, country music, alternative, pop, oldies, classical, jazz, faith based and local news.

When one examines radio, there is no one size fits all. The

audience that each station connects with is different. The differences are called '*demographics*' which describes the age, gender, ethnics and many other factors concerning every listening audience. So before venturing into radio advertising, it is important for the small business marketer to know something about the demographics of the people who buy your company's product and services.

For example if you are selling rooms at an assisted living community, you might find that advertising works best on an oldies, classical or even a religious station which report to have an older demographic audience. This might be more of your target audience than say an alternative, hard rock or pop music station which has a younger demographic audience. Or you might find through demographic research that your demographic audience is not the older demographics who use the service, but the middle age demographic group that helps their parents acquire such a facility.

Another example might be a company that specializes in water sports equipment. If they do not research their demographics, they may incorrectly assume their primary buying audience is younger audience only to discover that their larger purchases in boating equipment come from an older audience.

One could certainly advertise on each station that addresses a different demographic, however there is also the aspect of *how one delivers the message* to a particular demographic. Every target audience will respond to an advertising message differently. A sporting goods store that sells baseball equipment, swimming apparel and golfing supplies will need to consider a different demographic for each of those categories as their different products will appeal to different groups. These are just some of the things a small business marketer needs to consider with radio advertising.

In addition to all this is the cost. Every radio station has a different fee structure based on their draw and influence. The different times of day also impact price per ad.

So choosing a radios station has many aspects to consider. Here is a recap of those key points:

- Type of broadcast format

- Days, nights or weekends

- Time of day

- Demographics

- Message to that demographic audience

- Cost per ad

I will give you another example of an experience I had with radio advertising. I was advertising a stained and beveled glass studio in Atlanta. We wanted to experiment with radio advertising to reach a broader audience for our windows and doors.

Our first attempt was to buy a radio spot on a popular pop music station, as we wrongly assumed this was the station our demographics were listening to. We spent a lot of money and got no results. Then we switched to talk radio because the other owners and I liked talk radio and we wrongly assumed that this would be our target audience, because after all *we liked stained glass and talk radio.* This too was a dismal failure.

Around the time we were going to give up on radio we were contacted by an oldies station who heard our ads and they wanted to pitch us on using their radio station. I reluctantly set up an appointment and listened to their pitch. They were cheaper by 50% than the other two stations we tried, so I wrongly assumed they must have a weaker audience. Not wanting to blow another chunk of advertising money on a bulk of ads, I told the rep I would purchase 10 ads in their cheapest time slot which turned out to be the weekend. I would run it for one weekend, and it we got results, we would talk further. So we went to the station, produced an ad encouraged people to call for a 'free in home estimate' and ran it.

That weekend we were surprised to suddenly get calls right after the ad ran, but they were asking for appointments all over the metro area. Some were two hours away. Our sales staff was suddenly having scheduling problems and I had to take up some of the slack as the distances were so great that we had to cover. Then we also observed we were seeing some walk in traffic coming in from the ad. We ultimately made two sales that weekend directly from the radio, and lined up a 5 or 6 more in-home appointments following it.

The results were good, but we soon decided that the 'free in-home estimate' ad needed to go, as it was creating problems with scheduling and spreading us too thin. We learned the lesson that radio hits the audience all over, and we had to re-design our ad to get people to come to us, rather than us to them. Plus we had several appointments that our team went to but did not get a sale because these people calling for a free appointment were not as serious as ones that walked in. So we decided to do another weekend of ads. This time we changed them to directing people into the store, and emphasizing our location. With this final change, we had found our winning combination.

We discovered that we could generate walk-in traffic from radio on weekends by using this oldies station as this was the time they were at home working around the house and listening to the radio. We also discovered that our demographic was an oldies station listener, and they were the kind of people that dropped what they were doing and came in. It was light and easy music to listen to when working around the house, and usually was cheerful and the music seemed to hit many age groups. So we expanded our radio campaign and doubled the ads and ran them every weekend. I even met with the radio station sales rep and bought larger blocks of ads at an even lower rate by buying six months in advance, etc.

The radio station also threw in a lot of perks that helped us out too. They gave us prize patrols, one live broadcast a semester, radio station giveaways, sports tickets, included us in contests, etc. All of it turned into a great relationship that boomed our company sales into a whole new range. There were many lessons we learned with radio from this experience. What was most important was once one finds the right station, and the right advertisement, the magic can happen.

The Contents of a Good Radio Ad

When you advertise on radio, you are given typically a 30 second or 60 second spot, depending on how the radio station sells advertising. This may sound like a lot of time, but it runs out quickly when you are creating a commercial. There are many different schools of thought on the style of the commercial, and what works best. Does humor work better than rapid fire information? Does a serious commercial get more attention than a lighthearted one? I suppose it really depends on the marketing plan one is advancing as to whether it works for you.

However, there is a basic list of ingredients to follow to make sure your radio advertisement if effective in getting the listener to respond, setting aside artistic content and creation.

Here are the ingredients of a good radio ad:

- **Say the phone number 5X** - Repeat it with the complete area code and have it said at least five times during the course of the advertisement. This tends to 'ding in' the phone number into a listener's consciousness and compel them to dial if they have interest in what the ad says.

- **Make it clear what you are selling, promoting, offering, etc.** - If you are in the business of selling drapery in your store, make sure the ad relays this clearly. If you are promoting a sale in this ad, make sure that is prominent. If your company is promoting a service, make sure the service is clearly understood in the advertisement. This could mean repeating the product or service a few times, but more importantly make sure the listener connects clearly with what it is. Never be vague or coy on this.

- **If promoting a website, give the URL 5X** - Just like promoting a phone number, sometime the URL of a website is the key item you want to drive people to. Repeat this at least five times in the ad, and try to incorporate it into the wording of the ad to make it memorable. Example: *"Check out Georges fishing shop dot com... that's Georges fishing shop dot com... singing 'Georges fishing shop dot com'..."*

- **Give the address or location at least 2X** - If you are promoting a location and using the ad to drive people into the location, make sure the address is repeated at least twice. If you have time, do it three times. One can either repeat the address twice *'Come into our showroom at*

1204 Vermont Street in Des Moines...' or give a location such as *'Come see our showroom just 1½ block past the waterfront statue in downtown Sarasota...'*

- **Give the hours of operation** - If promoting a store location, give the hours of operation. If promoting a website, remind them they can shop it 24 hours a day. One car dealership uses the line *"Shop in your pajamas..."* to promote 24 hour a day shopping on the internet.

- **Say the name of the business 3X** - Repeat the name of the business three times in the ad if possible. If your business is the same name of the website, then make sure they get the connection. If you are promoting a store location, then the name of the business needs to be repeated, but not so much as the phone number.

- **Direct them to *do something*** - An advertisement should direct them to act. It should tell them to *go to a location, visit a website* or *call a number immediately.* Always make sure the message is consistent, and the direction you are giving them is unmistakably clear.

This is the list of key ingredients. It may sound like a lot of stuff to cram in 60 seconds of radio time, or even 30 seconds, but they are listed above in the order of importance. At a minimum people should walk away from having heard a radio ad with remembering your phone number or website in connection with what product or service you are selling.

If they miss the company name, hours of operation or location, this is not as bad as missing these first three. Do you see how that can work? If they really get the first three, they can and will connect. If you make hours of operation and company the most important, then they may or may not arrive in your store if they miss the address, website or phone number.

The most important information for a customer to retain from an advertisement on radio is:

- Phone number and/or website

- A connection the phone number (or website) together with an interest in your company's: product, service or event.

With these two they can arrive or connect with your company. Without them, your marketing '*turning that corner*' into becoming new customer income may or may not happen.

Artistic creation can also play into making the ad memorable, but never let artistic creation overwhelm getting your important aspects of the ad into the memory of the listener.

Television & YouTube

Television Advertising

Television advertising has changed over the years. To capture a viewer's attention and get them to act requires repetition. For the small business marketer, this can become an expensive endeavor. In the world of broadcasting, television statistically is falling farther and farther behind other forms of broadcasting such as radio and YouTube in terms of effectiveness. Since the 1970's with the expansion of cable and satellite television, the viewer has literally hundreds of channels at their disposal as well as the remote control for muting and switching channels.

To be successful in television advertising one has to become very creative. It is not going to be the successful tool for every business. However, there are certain broadcasts that people tend to leave on through commercial breaks and display ads on the screen. Some of these include sporting events, weather reports and movies.

If your target audience is one that might be in such a viewership, then the best recommendation is to study first what other advertisers are doing in the medium. Give the ones a direct call when you see an interesting ad and inquire as to how it is working for them. In other words, do not take the advertising salesman's word on it, but do your own homework by talking to the advertisers.

Local television shows can also be inexpensive on smaller cable stations for advertising, and they do reach a local viewership. You must also determine very much like radio the time of day in which to run your ads. The time frames that a majority of the viewership watches TV is called 'Primetime' which usually refers to 7pm to 11pm daily through the week, and sometimes on weekends.

The most effective form of advertisement on Television is to promote the phone number, location or website. One can have it visually displayed on the screen, but it is also important to repeat is in the audio portion of the broadcast as well. Quite often people turn on a television on a home environment and leave it playing in the background, so visuals can get missed. Factor in both audio and visual into your television ad.

YouTube

YouTube is one of the largest growing resources online for capturing a viewership. A small business marketer can create their own videos and post them on YouTube at no charge. One can create a channel on there for your business as well.

One of the most successful methods to employ the use of YouTube in marketing is to create 'How to' or 'Information' videos on how to use our companies products in every day settings. These types of videos do not need to be very extensive; in fact most of the ones that get a lot of views are the ones which are less than 10 minutes. One can also place links on the video, so that when people are watching and they want to go to your website they can click through. YouTube also allows videos to be monetized, and when a video reaches over 10,000 views it starts paying you for the video. It is not much, but in the long run every little bit helps to boost your marketing.

The more videos you post on the subject, the more you become the authority of that subject in the area. Having videos on YouTube also makes it easy to include them on your website which is another great way to tie your social media together with your other marketing efforts.

You can also email links as a way of answering client questions on a topic, and create a separate video to answer every one of the common questions people ask about your products and services.

The most important point about making these kinds of videos is to make them instructional, educational and informative. Overall it should be interesting and make people want to 'subscribe' to your channel. The better your content the easier it will be to create a following.

Visibility = Viability

There is a catchphrase that is a magic secret for any small business marketer who is marketing a storefront or business that depends on walk-in sales can use, and that is *'Visibility = Viability'.*

Remember that with all that you do in your set up, sales and lay out of your displays and storefront. When people can see your store this is a good thing. When people can see and read clearly your signage, that is an even better thing. When people can see your products this is an even greater thing. However, the greatest thing of all is when they can see the entire picture of your entire product image, and see it clearly, that is incredible marketing and success! If you can achieve massive visibility, you can achieve viability.

SET UP FOR VISIBILITY

In order to achieve success in this area, one must learn to look at their entire storefront and/or showroom setup and factor in visibility.

First we are going to examine a list of aspects of your store's visibility individually:

- Displays

- Products

- Signage

- Inside of the Store

- Overall Store Appearance

- People Working the Store

Then next thing we are going to do is to take the above list of aspects of your store, and plug each individual aspect into the first question below, and answer it and the five questions that follow it to help you improve upon the visibility of your store for each of the different aspects.

- When I stand back from the customer's perspective, can I see the _____ clearly?

- If 'yes' can I improve upon this further?

- If 'No' what is blocking it, or preventing it from being visible, and how can I change it?

- Can I answer 'yes' to the above from at least three different angles?

- If 'Yes' can I improve upon this further?

- If 'No' what needs to change to bring this to a 'Yes'?

Going through this exercise with your store set-up each time you attend a show will help you run a basic checklist on its visibility from the customer's viewpoint. Greater visibility makes for greater viability.

Improving visibility can mean adjusting displays so that one is not blocking the other or one is not too low, or too high. It can mean changing the color on a table cloth, or adjusting the angle of a sign to face the flows of body traffic in front of the store or business.

There can be many, many different and unique adjustments. One is trying to develop a particular viewpoint about improved visibility, and it takes a unique eye to see ones store this way. Too often one is so caught up into the set up, or 'this is how we have always done it' to take a moment and make an adjustment to improve visibility.

Every location of a store can present a unique set of variables that will make it different from the next store in the area. A store in a rural area or suburban area is different from a store on a downtown street. One might have trees in the way of one store, or a bend in the road that limits long range visibility for example. One can have a street sign or road medium in an urban setting that could potentially block visibility, or even another building or a curve in the road. An area with hills or slopes can make for an uneven set-up or walking path, impacting the visibility of the approach of the customer to your store.

Take nothing for granted, and always stand back and look at your store and run it through the visibility checklist at least once a month, as aspects of the community changes around a place of business and it is easy not to notice it. Make adjustments as needed, as sometimes it is the small thing that one adjusts that makes the biggest difference in sales.

Let's examine the different aspects listed above individually, and look at probably factors that can impact visibility with each one.

DISPLAYS

Displays can have their visibility be impacted from a variety of things. The direction it is positioned, the height it set at and even the level angle of the terrain upon which it sits. Color can also be a thing to adjust as well. A display set up on a pedestal or table will have a different light reflection than one set up on the floor or a shelf for example. This is why it is always a good idea to try different color table cloths with your table set ups, from light to dark to experiment with which one is going to be the most visible for your displays based on the setting of the store or showroom. This can also be a factor between indoor and outdoor displays as well.

Your neighbors of every business location will be different. Their displays adjacent to yours might impact the visibility of some of your displays. This is another reason to stand back and look at your visibility to maximize the impact with each unique set up.

Environment issues such as trees, lamp posts, trash cans, kiosk booths in a wide street, and even restaurants in close proximity can create lines of people at certain times of the day that can block or even increase visibility of your displays.

PRODUCTS

Visibility of your products can also be impacted by the same things listed above under displays. Sometimes one can look at their store and find a solution to improve the product visibility to compensate for a unique condition. One example may be to place your product higher to be seen over a crowd, such as an article of custom made clothing hanging from a pole, or a birdhouse on a pole. One birdhouse maker found out once from doing the visibility test came up with the idea for a future display to place a birdhouse in the shape of a mail box on a tall pole and paint on it 'Air Mail' and it became a new seller in this store, and also created more visibility from farther away when the street is crowded outside at rush hour. It all depends on the type of location one has for a storefront.

SIGNAGE

Signage is always the one item that can offer the greatest challenge to visibility. It is suggested when one is setting up their store that they consider sign placement in both high and low positions, as well as right and left facing different angles to make them visible from each possible direction. Large and small signs should be used as well. Signage shown from a distance should convey a simple message in large readable lettering, such as 'Portrait Artist', 'Printing Services' or 'Wood Furniture' etc.

The larger signage should be able to be not only be visible, but readable and convey a message that will invite the customer to find out more. Try to describe your products in four words or less if possible. Let your smaller signage when they are up close tell the larger story, your bigger signage should be more of a beacon drawing them in to find out more.

Neon signage also helps. The traditional 'Open' sign is an important basic in neon, but consider also one word signs such as names of products such as 'T-Shirts', 'Cell Phones' or 'Coffee'. There are also many forms of digital screens that change the message over and over again which can also help draw attention.

INSIDE OF THE STORE

When you walk through a commercial district, the stores that look more open and bright are the ones that seem to attract the most visitors. The ones that are closed up, dark and cluttered are not sufficiently visible. When you are looking at your store, and checking visibility on the inside from an exterior view, ask yourself if it appear inviting. Does it? A good view of the inside of your store, whether you have it set up to have customers come inside or not should have an inviting appearance which will create enough interest for the customer who is strolling and tired to come on over and see your storefront over others.

OVERALL STORE APPEARANCE

The overall appearance of your store should also be inviting on the outside and inside. Look at this as the final 'once over' the look at your stores 'Mojo'. Does it capture your attention from the visibility viewpoint? Can you see the displays, signage and product and know what your store is about at a glance when passing on the street? Does it invite you or intrigue to come inside? Can you see this from different angles? What is important in this step is that one knows the overall store is visible and inviting. Can you see it clearly? Does the appearance invite a passerby to enter? Is it interesting?

THE PEOPLE WORKING THE STORE

So often the people who work the store do not come into a business owner's equation in the marketing picture. However, sometimes this is all a customer sees as a first thing, not your product. Are they wearing appropriate clothing? Are they visible as being ones who are working the store from where they are standing, what they are doing, etc.? If they are sitting in the dark in the back of the store reading a book or playing with apps on a mobile phone, this is not being visible. This is invisible. Are they helping customers when they come inside? Are they crowding someone and not giving them space to look?

Make your people visible, along with all these other aspects of your store or make changes as needed. Some business owners go so far as to have the store or showroom staff wear uniforms or the same shirts or clothing items. Whatever you do, make it visible to the customer if you go this route. A store should look like people are manning it, and helping customers. Customers seeing others being helped and buying will do so themselves when the people manning a booth are visible. So make adjustments for this as well.

Overall we see that visibility equates to viability when one stands back and looks at their storefront or showroom from the viewpoint of the customer.

Doing this drill often can make the different in consistent sales. Have you ever made an adjustment to a sign in your store in the middle of a day for example, and observed customers responding to it and it improved sales? How many sales do you consider you missed before you made that adjustment?

Doing this little visibility step right at the beginning of the day can impact your overall sales, especially on a weekend, and conservatively one could say it might even boost your sales by as much as 10% to 25% over time.

It can make a huge difference, because a customer who passes your store because there is so much else to see, and your store is invisible from a particular angle or aspect to them from the direction they are coming from could cost you a sale.

Find creative ways to make your storefront and showroom visible to customers to draw them in!

VISIBILITY ONLINE

Making your products visible on the internet through websites and blogs is another great way to promote your business. Small business marketers can also set up point of purchase websites to sell products and other creations right online. An important point to consider in doing so is licensing, especially if your business is original art work.

LICENSING

Licensing one's work if it is original art work is a great way to expand sales and generate additional income from your art. 'Licensing' refers to selling the rights to use your artwork or design for a defined period and percentage of the sales income. Instead of simply selling your originals or selling your designs outright, many artists will grant the right (license) to use their art on a specific product, for a set time period in exchange for a percentage of the income generated by the sales. This percentage is called a 'royalty'.

By licensing your art, you have the potential to earn income on the same art piece or collection several times over. It can become a form of residual passive income if your designs gain popularity. It is also a great way to expand name recognition as an artist, and reach larger markets with your designs and creations. Here are some useful websites to review and learn more about licensing your art:

ArtLicensingInfo.com

ArtofLicensing.com

ArtLicensingBlog.com

There are also numerous art licensing agents to be found online, and it is advisable to compare several before committing to one particular firm. One can also find reading books to read on this as well which will cover the basics.

Identity Capturing

The biggest successful action for a small business marketer is to have a system in place in their business operation that enables them to practice identity capturing. *What is identity capturing?* It is the collecting of your customer's names, addresses and phone numbers who buy from you and also in this modern day their email addresses! It also includes capturing the identities of people who visited your store, and did not buy. *What do you know about these people?* They have some kind of interest in your business!

So many small businesses exist exclusively on point of purchase sales from their store, and do not even think to capture names of the people who buy from them. *Why is capturing these names important?* Essentially, this is important because it provides you with a resource to reach out to them again in the future as well as by other means and sell them more products and services. Your best customer and easiest one to sell is the one whom has already made a purchase from you!

So capturing identities enables you to create a system where you can build relationships with former clients, and produce more sales. So therefore, identity capturing requires also the additional step of following up with them for future purchases. So this really becomes a two part process. Capturing the identity and creating a system that enables you to follow up. So let's explore both of these points in detail.

IDENTITY CAPTURING AS A ROUTINE PRACTICE

What are the best ways to capture your buyer's identity? To begin, you have to have a storefront or even a booth at a public trade show or arts and crafts show. To take on such an activity, must be able and willing to talk to people, and engage them in conversation to a greater or lesser degree. Identity capturing is not something that one successfully accomplishes by placing it on automatic. You have to be willing to talk to people, and encourage them to give you their information.

The first thing you have to ask yourself is: how valuable a list of names would be to you that consisted entirely customers that had made a purchase from you or were familiar with your work? What price would you put on a list of 100, 200 or even 500 names of those types of people?

While you are considering the answer to that question, let's examine some methods to capture people's identities at an arts and crafts show or home show, as these types of shows are common in a community and offer booths that can give a local small business some additional exposure over a one to three day period.

The fish bowl giveaway

The easiest way to start with identity capturing is to place a bowl on your table that allows people to place their business card or contact information written on a piece of paper into it. The draw for them doing this is usually best done with some sort of giveaway item, usually one of the more desirable items in your booth. In order for this to work, the giveaway item has to be something people want, so you will want to giveaway an item that is one of your most popular pieces and in high demand. To enter into this contest, inform them that the winner will be notified through phone or email, so make sure they also include that on their slip of paper.

If you do this throughout the show, you will capture names and identities of a lot of people who are your customers and people who have just seen your booth who become your future prospects. The value of this second group of people is that they attend arts and crafts shows, so they could become a future customer for you at a later show if you stay in touch. One cannot stay in touch if you do not have their contact information to do so, so try a giveaway to capture it!

The sign-up sheet

This can be a simple pad of paper that you keep on the table and ask people who purchased or engaged you in conversation to sign up on. This can even be prospects that did not buy for whatever reason, but you still encourage them to sign up for a giveaway contest you are doing or just to 'sign up for our newsletter to find out about our next shows' or 'get the latest news happening with our store'.

This second one of asking them to 'sign up for a newsletter' works for those artists that have such a unique product that they literally have fans who are in awe of their work, and may buy more again in the future. This second approach to 'sign up for a newsletter' may not work as well for booths built around smaller impulse buy items, so in that case I would recommend doing the giveaway to capture names always.

Note: When you provide any sign-up sheet, always write a bogus name in the first line with a name, address, phone number and email address. For some reason, people will commonly avoid being the first to sign such a list, but will willingly sign if others have done so. I suppose it appears safe to do so if others have gone there first.

The guest book

This is similar to the basic sign-up sheet, but a little more of a formal approach. This is where you buy one of those professional guest books used at weddings or other special occasions, and have it sitting on an easel inside your store or near the entrance where people who visit can sign up their names.

You can tie this in with a giveaway of an item or free service if you wish. This approach is a classy way of saying 'give me your name and contact info' and works well for the specialty artists who create larger more expensive works.

Note: When you provide any guest book, always write a fake name in the first line with a name, address, phone number and email address. Just like the basic sign-up sheet, people will commonly avoid being the first to sign such a list, but will willingly sign if others have done so before them.

Live Internet sign-up

If you are at a show where you have electric power and can arrange internet access, you can also set up a sign-up form where people can sit down and take a survey or enter a contest by filling out information right in your store or show booth online, and this captures their identity. You do not see this often at outdoor arts and crafts shows, but sometimes at indoor trade shows this is much easier to do.

It is not a common practice now, but it is a practice done at a lot of professional trade shows and so I thought I would include this here for those small business marketers that are also computer savvy and interested in trying this approach. It may become a common practice in the future as technology evolves, so it is worth considering and exploring. I will go into more on this further down in this chapter, however, this makes for a paperless lead capturing approach right in your business and it can save a lot of time.

If you set something like this up, it works best to have several computers or another means for paper lead capturing that you are using as well, as people can be slow in entering info on a computer. This can be a great set up for an indoor trade show.

The nudge

If you have the luxury of having a few extra volunteers helping you with your storefront or booth, it is always a good idea to assign at least one or two of them the task of identity capturing by having them man the station where you have a sign-up form or drawing, and have them nudge people who come to the booth to enter. I have found that setting up a contest bowl or offering any kind of sign-up sheet does not mean that people will automatically enter their name; in fact most will not do so unless prompted. My best advice is to have someone who is the most dynamic or 'willing to talk to people' personality to be responsible for this job at your booth.

At professional trade shows, they usually select the prettiest young girl, or handsome young man to perform this role. If you do not have such a person helping you, that is okay. Choose a young child who is cute and willing to talk to people, or anyone who is can be irresistible to people so they will not say no. Most anyone can become good at this role if one practices. It takes the willingness to charm people, flatter them, tease them or just be overtly friendly to them and repeatedly ask people to sign-up all throughout the show.

Costumed characters

At some arts and crafts shows and trade shows vendors use a costumed character to perform the duty of asking for sign-ups. If it is a full body costumed suit, often the person wearing it does not have to do anything other than gesture to the sign up book, bowl or list and act like a character. You can get away with a lot as a costumed character, and it is a great draw for kids. People love to have their picture taken with a costumed character.

The person wearing the suit should give out high-fives, hugs and basically be larger than life without getting too caught up in the role to forget the sign-up sheet, book or contest. Doing the costumed character stunt works best on cooler days, and ones that are not likely to get someone caught in the rain. Doing this on a hot July day at a show can really limit a person's time in a full body costume, as they can get quite warm and it is akin to walking around with a sleeping bag all over your body, even if they are ventilated and have a built-in fan. A better costume for a hot day is to dress like a clown, pirate or some other character that does not require a full body suit.

Creativity is the magic

One can get creative as one would wish with identity capturing, and there certainly can be many ways to do this. What you are trying to obtain is the customer or prospects name, phone number, address and email address. Quite honestly if you can at least get a name and email address, you can turn these lists into a gold mine for future shows and sales for you. If you find it too complicated or slow to ask for all of their contact info, one should then simply focus on going for just the name and email. With those to basic pieces of information you can do a lot with future promotions.

FOLLOW UP

The value and return from the efforts of identity capturing comes from having a system in place for follow up. There are many ways to do this, and any artist should have at least some system in place for contacting people again.

Now let's examine some of the various ways to do this from the very simple, to the more automated and sophisticated. All are easy to do, if you are willing to take the time to stay organized with it. It is well worth the advantage it can give you in future sales.

The very simple, non-computer method

Some business marketers are not computer savvy at all, and need a basic system to be able to contact their former customers and prospects without using a computer. Today, there are some very simple ways to do this with just keeping paper records.

The easiest and least technically complicated way will require that you at least own or have access to a copy machine, and know how to use one. You can purchase brands of mailing labels (example: Avery labels), and in those boxes of labels there is usually a black and white template of which you can make copies of and use to hand write in or type with a typewriter the names and addresses of the identities you have captured.

From this you can build a master list, and one that you can make copies of using the mailing labels and have a means to mail these people information about your business. Keep hand writing or typing onto your list and expand your files on each and every show, and keep these as your master list. Whenever you want to send out a mailing, you can simply use a copy machine and copy these names onto labels and peel off and attach these printed labels to your mailing.

If you want to send out a newsletter or postcard to let people know about your business or showroom, you can coordinate with a local printing company to make these items for you or hand draw them out yourself and use your copy machine to print them onto postcard stock paper. Then cut them into postcards or fold them into newsletter and mail them with postage attached.

This is perhaps the most basic approach for those who are not familiar with computers, but certainly not the most cost effective one. Paper, printing and postage mailing can be more expensive over time to use for this style of marketing, and due to cost can mean that you cannot afford to do this frequently. However, it is it a very non-technical way to go about it, and is better than having no system in place.

Computer lead capturing methods

If you have some basic working knowledge of how to use a home computer or the internet, there are a lot of ways to manage your lists and make contacting your people very easy.

The first would be to get a copy of the program Excel from Microsoft, and learn to use it. You can set up a template and manually enter names into a master list and use this list to export them to a mailing label format and print mailers as needed. There are also several other lead management software services you can sign up for online that will enable you to do this as well, and here are a few you can explore:

www.constantcontact.com

www.printmanager.com

www.freelancetech.com

The next and perhaps the most low cost and easiest way to manage leads and stay in contact is to exclusively focus on names and email addresses, and send out email newsletters and reminders of upcoming shows.

This is best done in coordination with having your own website too, that way you can put your website on all of your contact information and people who you miss capturing as an identity can perhaps visit your website later on in the privacy of their own home, and sign up for your newsletter if they wish.

Once you have a website set up, you will want to sign up or a separate service that allows you to manage email list and create your own newsletters. If you search on the internet, you can find several companies that provide you with this service. They provide you with a link or 'widget' once you set up your account with them that you can add to your website and capture leads and identities from there, but also enable you to enter names onto your list that you captured from your shows and manage your lists.

The email management service I recommend because it is user friendly is:*mailchimp.com* because they enable you to tag your lists into groups, which can work great for you to email former customers if you group them into shows you attended. When you return to that show, you can send out an advanced email and remind them to come see you again.

MailChimp.com is entirely free up to lists of 2000 and then they begin to charge you a low monthly rate for the service. A mailing list of 2000 would be quite an achievement for an arts and crafts show vendor artist, and it one is using a list that large, certainly one is making money with it and can afford the additional fees. Until you reach that size, it is an awesome way to stay organized for free.

Using your identities captured with awesome follow up tricks

Newsletters: Services like ***www.mailchimp.com*** have platforms where one can create a newsletter, and custom sign up forms that you can add to your website. A newsletter can be created months ahead of time, and set up to automatically be sent to your list on specified dates. Your mailing list can be working for you by means of pre-set automated advanced emails even when your business is closed.

 While at shows: When you have names from a show that your business is at, you may want to enter them into your mailing database after each show. This way you can constantly build upon a master and even sub-lists and stay organized with it.

With online access, you can even go back to your hotel room or your home base the evenings you are at an overnight show and enter the identities you collected that day. Send all of your daily visitors an exclusive coupon for the next day, and see if you can get them back for additional purchases.

- **Coupons:** With any identity collection and follow up program, always think with rewarding everyone who signs up. Make them all winners by giving them a coupon to use for a discount on your website, or at your place of business. Invite them to give this coupon to their friends, and email it to them.

- **Advanced reminders:** Once you have collected names, you can email people in advance letting them know the next trade, business or other type of show you are going to be at. At first you can email your entire list, and keep them all notified. If you are traveling around and doing several shows, you might want to sort out the names by the show, region or State you captured it in and send out advanced emails to your 'Georgia' or 'Florida' customers for example. Once a list grows, you can selectively mail reminders to groups by staying organized with mailing list management software.

You can even used advanced reminders to tell customers about upcoming sales, promotions or specials at your place of business. You can send reminders about back to school or the holiday shopping too.

SUMMARY

When one is looking at the subject of identity capturing and follow up, there are systems for every small business marketer depending on what they are willing to do. The most important thing to remember is that identity capturing is important, and even if you do not have a computer, or the time to learn. Then all identities should have a system in place to follow up. One should have at least a basic system working that you expand on later or hire someone to manage for you. The best system to have is one that works for you. Any system is better than no system.

So how much is a list of customer names and prospects that have seen your product to you? If you read this chapter, you are probably realizing the income potential from such a list. What has been presented here is a low cost way for you to obtain the information.

Certainly one has the expense of the item one is giving away, and the costs involved in setting up follow up systems, but the return on this investment into the future can be huge. Having a point of purchase system online that is connected to your business website can help you make sales 24 hours a day, 7 days a week. They can also drive business into your physical location.

Finding Places Where the Competition is *Not*

An important skill to develop as a small business marketer is that keen sense of observation where one can identify where their competition is not visible. Going through your community and marketplace as a small business marketer is one way to research this. Another way is to collect information on where you competition is advertising and marketing their company. The ultimate goal is to find places where your competition is not and grab the spotlight.

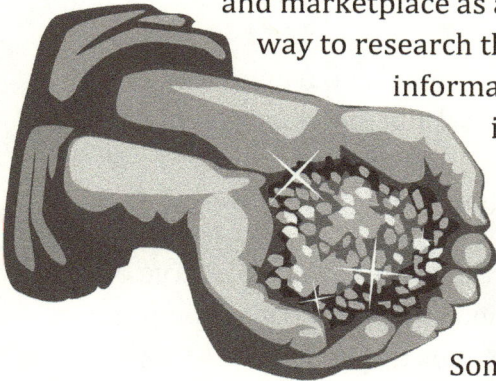

Sometimes it is in the most unique and unexpected place that one can get that edge over the competition and become visible to the prospective client. As an example there once a home remodeler that I came across that wanted to stand out in the community and draw attention to his company beyond the signs he had on all his vans. He wanted to double his exposure in the community in a way that would get his phone ringing.

He began placing signs in the yards of all the homes he had done work on (getting permission from his customers first) and this helped to increase the presence around town. However, he was still looking something more visible though out town. Later while driving around town one day he was stuck in traffic behind a yellow taxi cab. He got the idea to contact the company and ask them about advertising on their cabs.

When he called he found out that by coincidence that the owner of the company had ordered small signs to mount on top of all the cabs in their fleet. This is a common practice in larger cities like New York and Chicago, but in our smaller community it was not being done yet. So the contractor purchased ad space on all of their taxi cabs, and within a week he had doubled the presence of his company all over the city. It was a new and unique campaign so people took notice, and his phone began to ring constantly.

So the above is an example of ideas this one business owner found that enabled him to gain a position in the market place where his competition was not. He was observant and constantly thinking about new ways to reach his target audience.

As another example, there was a time when I was in charge of my company marketing of a stained and beveled glass door and window manufacturing company. Our target audience was homeowners that lived in homes valued above $250,000 or more. The higher valued the home, the more likely they were to purchase our product. We knew this from statistical data, and so we could plot out neighborhoods to target.

I tried print advertising in every newspaper in town and had little or no success. I had an effective direct mail campaign to these neighborhoods, and this seemed to be the best tool in our arsenal, but I was looking for more ways to reach people and increase our visibility.

I found it in the most unexpected place ever. One of my customers was self-publishing a small community newsletter out of her house that was circulated in the neighborhood of 100 to 150 homes once a month.

They used this newsletter to remind people about everything from homeowner's association issues, to local events at the nearby schools, things happening in the neighborhood, etc. My client asked if we would purchase an ad and help offset the costs. They wanted $15 for the ad, so I paid for a ¼ page ad and put a photo of an entry door system we made in the ad and our address and phone number offering a free in home estimates, etc. I did not think much of it, as I was doing it more as an effort to help her out that receive business.

Within the following week of the ad running in that small subdivision of 100-150 homes we received 6 appointments, and sold 4 complete entry systems grossing over $25,000 in new orders. We ran the ad again the next month, and got two more orders of around $10,000. So with a total of $30 invested so far we had returned over $35K for our business. This is an amazing return of marketing dollars invested by anyone's standards. So I of course began to look for ways to strengthen and build upon this idea.

We of course ran ads for every issue in that subdivision newsletter and continued to until I sold the business a few years later. However, we capitalized on this idea by offering a discount of 30% to our entire list of customers in our mailing list on any stained glass lamp in our store inventory for any customer who brought in a copy of their own neighborhood newsletter. We also offered a small free gift if they did not want a lamp. The newsletters began coming in. We discovered that there were other subdivisions around town that had similar publications with their homeowners associations. Many of them were actively seeking advertisers to offset costs, and were happy to sell us ad space cheap.

Clients would bring us the newsletter, get their discount and we would call the association newsletter and buy an ad. They were always very affordable, and almost one for one would get us a new order in that neighborhood as soon as we ran the ad the first time. This was an amazing and simple way we found to reach new clients a get phenomenal return for a low advertising investment.

These small publications were personal and unique to a target audience, and the ad showing up in there was almost a recommendation as the more we ran them the more others consulted with their neighbors and the appointments came in. With the age of the internet, these kinds of newsletters are giving way to email newsletters, etc.

However there may still be neighbors willing to publish them if they are funded, so it does remain a possibility that this kind of campaign could work for any kind of home improvement company even today.

As a small business marketer you have to be willing to explore those unique positions in the market place and test it for results. Sometimes you come across something that just sounds crazy, but if you do not try it you will never know if it works. Sometimes crazy can be way out of budget to, so it is recommended that if you are going to test to do so with small increments of money invested. This is the safest way to test the untried whenever possible.

There are many unique positions one could seize in the market place. Some may work for your business and some may not.

Here is a list of unusual and unique places to advertise:

- Taxi cab advertisements

- Pizza delivery boxes

- Movie theatre pre-movie slide shows

- Placemats in popular local restaurants

- Any youth sports team uniforms

- Billboards at the ballpark

- Refrigerator magnets

- Airline magazines and tray tables

- Bathroom stalls

- Free mouse pads

- CAPTCHA ads online (Google 'CAPTCHA ads' for more info)

- The floor of a grocery store or other retail store

- The bottom of a public swimming pool

- Zambonis at the ice rink

- Print your logo or ad on the seat bottom of women's sweat pants

- Sewer covers

- Ads inside video games

- The sides of buildings

- The sides of vending machines

- Plastic bags given away at trade shows

- Coffee or drink cups given away at public events

- The sides of city buses

- Engraved bricks as part of a monument or sidewalk

- Dog sweaters

- Horse blankets

- Aerial banner towing behind airplanes

If you take some time to get your creative juices flowing, you may be surprised at the places you find to advertise. As a small business marketer, sometimes the most unique position is the one that will give you the distinction.

In Atlanta, Georgia during the 1991 & 1992 Braves seasons, I witnessed a unique rise of one small business marketer. He was the co-owner of a BBQ restaurant in a small town in Roswell. He took an old red VW van and mounted a large pink pig on the top, and drove it all over the Atlanta metro area. He even set up a BBQ grill at Atlanta Fulton County Stadium tailgating before the Braves playoff games. During the World Series when the Braves played the Minnesota Twins, he flew the van with the pig up to Minneapolis and participated in the tailgating there too.

He made national news on CNN and all the Atlanta television stations because he was the only restaurant to pull off such a stunt from Georgia. His gimmick was more than just serving Georgia BBQ at the World Series opponent of the Braves; he captured a national spotlight in doing so. All during this time his restaurant was always jamb packed day in and day out at home during lunch and dinner traffic.

I later ran into him some months after this incident and asked him how he pulled it off. He said the cargo flight to Minnesota cost him around $1000 for the air freight, but he got millions in dollars in free prime time TV coverage in doing so. Talk about making the most of one's advertising dollars!

This is the perfect example of original thinking and looking for the place your competition was not. He got free news local coverage at the Atlanta games, alongside other restaurants doing similar things at the tailgate party. However, when he pulled off flying the pig van show up in Minnesota his free media exposure was launched into a whole new orbit.

As a small business marketer, one must develop a creative, watchful eye and let one's imagination soar sometimes to put one's own business into the spotlight where your competition is not.

Tying All the Marketing in Together

To orchestrate an effective marketing campaign a small business marketer needs to build all aspects of the campaign one upon the other. All the individual parts of a campaign need to tie together. Each separate action needs to connect to the other in some way, to capture the prospective customer's interest and sell them your products and services and then retain them as a client for the long haul.

Let's assume that your website will be the central core of your campaign. This will act as your online source for information, interaction with your customers, storefront and general point of contact information. With this in mind as the central point of the campaign, then all other aspects of your campaign should refer to the website in some way.

The following items you create for your campaign should have your website URL listed on it, references to it or connected to it with a direct link.

- Business Cards

- You Blog(s)

- You advertising both online and print

- News press releases

- Direct Mail cards & letters

- Signage in all forms

- Radio ads should mention it

- Social Media pages

- Your email signature

Your website at the same time should call attention to your radio ads, blogs, social media pages with individual links, your phone number and your email (as a link). If you post online or print any articles always include the website URL and the other URL's of your blogs, etc.

Your store location can also be an important factor of a marketing campaign if you are in retail. It could be the central point of where all your marketing leads, and thus the address and map directing people to get there should be published in all possible places online and in print.

Your hold button at the office should play messages for the callers on hold. These messages should mention the website, blogs and even play running radio ads to keep campaigning to the person while they are waiting. If you have a television ad or other video you might also play that on your website or in your showroom in continual loop.

Once one begins to think with all the forms of marketing connecting, it is easy to see how it all becomes a complex net designed to capture attention.

An important way to tie all the marketing together is to have a campaign slogan, theme and/or tag line. This can be a color coordinated theme with a message and a logo.

Take some time and examine some of the biggest known organizations and companies and see if you can list out all the elements of their marketing campaign. Take the Detroit Tigers baseball team for a moment. They have a logo with the old English 'D' that is placed on all their merchandise promoting the team. It is on their website, their uniforms, press releases, letters, tickets, etc. They also have a color coordinated theme of blue and orange and also white. They have a popular tag line too: *"Always a Tiger"*.

All the major sports teams have this marketing machine in place, and all of their marketing connects with the rest. Some of the biggest most successful sports franchises in terms of marketing merchandise are the Washington Redskins, Dallas Cowboy and New York Yankees. These sports franchises are near the top of all merchandising franchises because their marketing machine can tie it all together.

Many large corporations follow the same pattern. Look at Apple, McDonalds, Burger King, Avis, Coca-Cola, Southwest Airlines, Kellogg's, etc. Explore how they tie all their marketing together to see the pattern. Then look at medium to small sized companies in your region and see which ones are really prospering. Which ones have the public name recognition in your local marketplace? Which ones have a marketing campaign that is consistent and continuing?

These are the ones to study and model your efforts after. They can even be in a totally unrelated business to your own. What is important is that you study the framework of what they are doing and attempt to mimic it as best that you can. The easiest pair of boots to follow are the ones worn by a successful one.

A Simple 10 Step Marketing Plan

If you have gone through this book up to this point and made notes of things you want to explore or implement into your marketing strategies, now is the time to begin creation of your own plan.

A marketing plan as you can see can and should be multifaceted, but at the same time consistent.

The recommended approach for launching a basic campaign is a 10 step plan which costs very little to do:

1. Discover and isolate what your company's unique position is in the market. What makes you different, unique or better than any other business offering similar goods and services? Survey your customers or prospective customer base and find out what they respond to, what makes them interested in your product or services, etc. This is perhaps the most important step of the entire campaign.

2. Come up with a consistent message that you can brand your company with. This can also include a logo or icon along with a written slogan or message.

3. Build your social media profiles for your company pages

on Facebook, Twitter, Linkedin and Pinterest. Tie this in with your website, and other print media.

4. Build a website tying in all your social media.

5. Prepare basic promotional items for immediate use. This would include any printed material needed and business cards. Make sure your business cards promote your website and social media.

6. Join groups within your community and begin regular attendance and participation.

7. Begin blogging about your company's products and services and how it relates to the community, etc. Tie the blog in with your website, and promote it through your social media pages.

8. Host an event at your place of business. Invite members of the community, and use it to promote your products and services. Include some public speakers. Make sure your signage is in place and people can easily find your location. If you operate a business that does not have a store or showroom, then consider renting a hotel conference or meeting space and host your event there including signage, etc.

9. Purchase some basic online ads after your Facebook page has grown to the point where you have your vanity URL established. Promote your business page and website in the advertisement.

10. Create some videos about your using your products and services and post them on YouTube, creating your own company channel. Promote your videos and channel on your other social media and your website.

Once you have completed this 10 step plan, you can build upon it with other larger marketing practices such as larger events, radio advertising, a direct mail campaign and self publishing a book.

Launching a marketing campaign does not need to be costly or burdensome. It does require some advanced preparation which can involve time.

One certainly can hire out some of the services for things one does not want to do such as setting up a website or blog, or designing a logo, etc.

The main point as a small business marketer is that one use your imagination, and creativity and put together a campaign that is unique and surveyed so that it hits your target audience. Surveying what your customers will respond to is essential, and a preliminary step as defined in step one. If you do this step well the rest of the steps are easy.

This is a simple 10 step plan. It was designed not to overwhelm you, but to show you it does not have to be difficult. Follow it and you will have launched a good foundation on which the rest of your marketing can be built upon.

Remember it is important to design your plan to continually show up in your target markets field of vision as often as possible, repeating this over and over again wherever they look.

This is the 'multifaceted approach' this book lays out for you. Do as many of these things shown in this book as you can, and find and discover your own as well. Always look for new ways to draw in customers.

Never become complacent with what you are doing, and be always ready to try something new, especially with the ever-changing internet. If you can do this and do it well, you will succeed.

Summary

Throughout this book many approaches have been addressed to help the small business marketer achieve success. To some readers, portions of these techniques or suggestions may not be new. To others the book and its information have been seen as a revelation and it has helped them market their businesses effectively.

As with any book I have written on marketing or management, it all comes down to application. The individual who reads the material needs to go out and apply the material to see if it works for them. One can only take the scholarly approach for so long. At some point the material needs to be simply put into use.

As an author I have tried to impart within these pages the small business marketing nuggets of information that I have learned through sometimes expensive lessons, in hopes to help someone else avoid the long path and help them get onto the short path to success. What I have presented here I have found works. It may

not work for everyone, and I do not have any delusions that they will *all* work for *everyone*. So examine each nugget for usefulness and apply what will work for you and your company.

I have always considered the small business to be the backbone of every economy, and without them there would be no commerce, culture or even a civilization. So if you have read this book and enjoyed it, I hope that you apply what you have learned and become a successful marketer. Any boost I can give to the small business will improve the lives of the people that business comes into contact with.

I hope you will also take time to share this book with others and follow up by writing a positive review online to encourage others to avail themselves of this information also. I wish you nothing but continued success and prosperity. As a final note, I am always happy to hear from my readers, so please feel free to contact me if you have any questions.   You can contact me through my personal website at:

www.michaeldelaware.com

In the future I intend to include forums on this website where we can share ideas and work together to find new ways to become successful.

Reference Section

Here is a list of some Social Media entities. This is by no means a complete list:

Twitter.com

Facebook.com

YouTube.com

LinkedIn.com

Flickr.com

Delicious.com

Pinterest.com

FourSquare.com

Yelp.com

Digg.com

Last.fm

StumbleUpon.com

TwitPic.com

Vimeo.com

Spotify.com

Tumblr.com

LibraryThing.com

MySpace.com

SocialVibe.com

Technorati.com

DeviantART.com

DesignFloat.com

LiveJournal.com

MegaVideo.com

Reddit.com

Audioboo.fm

Skype.com

Wordpress.com

Blogger.com

FriendFeed.com

Hyves.nl

Bebo.com

Typepad.com

Xing.com

Grooveshark.com

Lockerz.com

Google+

Buzz.com

Dopplr.com

Playfire.com

SoundCloud.com

Wakoopa.com

Blogster.com

For more social media entities go to *Wikipedia.org* and search 'Social Networking Websites' and you will find a more extensive list.

Here is a list of some other scheduling websites for social media:

Twuffer.com

Bufferapp.com

SproutSocial.com

StreamSend.com

LaterBro.com

Twaitter.com

FutureTweets.com

About the Author

Michael Delaware is a Phoenix, Arizona native who now resides in Battle Creek, Michigan with his wife Margarita. He also lived in Georgia for 15 years in the 1980's and 1990's where he owned and operated a stained and beveled glass studio in the Metro-Atlanta area. During those years he was an active volunteer in the community, coordinating annual Arts and Crafts Festivals in the downtown district of Roswell, Georgia. He also participated in Arts & Crafts Shows for over 25 years as a vendor in numerous States. He has been a Michigan resident since 1999.

His other published works include numerous non-fiction books on real estate, sales management, marketing and other self-help topics. He has also published fiction and non-fiction stories for children

As an illustrator and photographer, he has included his works in his own books and blogs. He enjoys hiking and mountain biking in the great outdoors and taking long walks in the woods with his dog.

Currently he is an active Realtor in Michigan and frequent community volunteer. He is a member of the National Association of Realtors, The Council of Residential Specialists, and the Michigan Association of Realtors. He is also an active member of the Battle Creek Area Association of Realtors where he was awarded 'Realtor of the Year' in 2010, and served as Board President in 2011. He founded his own independent publishing company in 2012.

To follow Michael:

www.MichaelDelaware.com

Facebook.com/MichaelDelawareAuthor

Goodreads.com/MichaelDelaware

Amazon.com/Author/MichaelDelaware

Linkedin.com/in/MichaelDelaware

@MichaelDelaware

Other titles by the author

available as eBooks:

The Art of Sales Management: Lessons Learned on the Fly *(also available in print)*

The Art of Sales Management: Revelations of a Goal Maker *(also available in print)*

The Art of Sales Management: 75 Training Drills to Build Confidence, Excellence & Teamwork *(also available in print)*

Arts & Craft Shows: The Top 10 Mistakes Vendor Artists Make… *And How To Avoid Them! (also available in print)*

Arts & Crafts Shows: 12 Secrets Every Artist Vendor Should Know *(also available in print)*

Inspiration: The Journey of a Lifetime

For Real Estate:

Understanding Land Contract Homes: In Pursuit of the American Dream

Land Contract Homes for Investors

Going Home… Renting to Home Ownership in 10 Easy Steps

In Children's Fiction:

Scary Elephant Meets the Closet Monster

In Children's Non-Fiction:

My Name is Blue: The Story of a Rescue Dog

More titles will be available in print in late 2013 and in 2014.
For a current list of available print books visit:

www.ifandorbutpublishing.com

If, And or But
Publishing Company

www.ingramcontent.com/pod-product-compliance
Lightning Source LLC
Chambersburg PA
CBHW022055210326
41519CB00054B/434